RAISE YOUR EBENEZER

A Field Guide to Suffering

RAISE YOUR EBENEZER

A Field Guide to Suffering

Dr. Ted Goshorn

Advocate Press

South Carolina United Methodist Advocate Press, Columbia, South Carolina
Copyright © 2024 by South Carolina United Methodist Advocate Press

All scripture, unless otherwise quoted, is taken from the New Revised Standard Version Updated Edition (NRSVUE), Copyright © 2021 National Council of Churches of Christ in the United States of America. Used by permission. All rights reserved worldwide.

Scripture quotations marked (NVI-PT) are taken from Biblia Sagrada, Nova Versão Internacional®, NVI® Copyright © 1993, 2000 by Biblica, Inc.™ Used by permission. All rights reserved worldwide.

Scripture quotations marked (KJV) is taken from the King James Bible (public domain).

All rights reserved. No part of this book may be reproduced or transmitted in any form or by any means, electronic or mechanical, including photocopying, recording or by any information storage and retrieval system, without permission in writing from the publisher.

First published in the United States of America in 2024

Library of Congress Cataloging-in-Publication Data
Raise Your Ebenezer
p. cm.

ISBN 978-1-966237-05-1

To my family,
Dana, Jackson, and Carter,
whose love so reflects God's love

and

To Graham Snyder,
whose "southern drawl" suggestion to write
through my suffering inspired this book.

Table of Contents

Beginning the Journey
Chapter 1: Introduction 3
Chapter 2: How to Trust God 13

Part 1: Getting Acquainted
Chapter 3: Expect Hardship..25
Chapter 4: Expect Change 33
Chapter 5: Expect to Lose Security...............................41
Chapter 6: Expect Relational Disruption.....................51
Chapter 7: Expect Fear..63
Chapter 8: Expect a Valley Experience.........................73
Chapter 9: Expect Divine Empathy..............................83
Chapter 10: Expect Something Good...........................93

Part 2: Survival Strategies
Chapter 11: Lean on Friends 107
Chapter 12: Be a Friend 121
Chapter 13: Practice Examen to Wait Well................131
Chapter 14: Do Things that Bring Joy.......................139
Chapter 15: Look to the Past and Give Thanks 151
Chapter 16: Practice Forgiveness 161
Chapter 17: Pray with Emotional Honesty................171
Chapter 18: Go to Nature 181
Chapter 19: Focus on what Matters............................191
Chapter 20: Raise Your Ebenezer................................201

Part 3: Discovering Hope
Chapter 21: Find the Light...213
Chapter 22: Conclusion: God Empowers Us.............221

Afterword..231
Appendix 1: Short of Breath from Life's Exhaustion 235
Appendix 2: Thanksgiving Worksheet.......................237
Notes 241

Beginning the Journey

Come, thou Fount of every blessing, tune my heart to sing thy grace;
streams of mercy, never ceasing, call for songs of loudest praise.
Teach me some melodious sonnet, sung by flaming tongues above.
Praise the mount! I'm fixed upon it, mount of thy redeeming love.

Here I raise mine Ebenezer; hither by thy help I'm come;
and I hope, by thy good pleasure, safely to arrive at home.
Jesus sought me when a stranger, wandering from the fold of God;
he, to rescue me from danger, interposed his precious blood.

O to grace how great a debtor daily I'm constrained to be!
Let thy goodness, like a fetter, bind my wandering heart to thee.
Prone to wander, Lord, I feel it, prone to leave the God I love;
here's my heart, O take and seal it, seal it for thy courts above.

—Robert Robinson, 1758

Chapter 1

Introduction

"Then Samuel took a stone and set it up between Mizpah and Jeshanah and named it Ebenezer, for he said, 'Thus far the Lord has helped us.'"
—*1 Samuel 7:12*

Just outside of Albuquerque sits the Petroglyphs National Monument. My family and I came to see drawings made by inhabitants of the land long ago. At this point, we had yet to see drawings but were enjoying the sunshine and the terrific views of Albuquerque. As we turned down a path, we saw many little stone monuments. They were small, maybe six inches to a foot high, and definitely human-made: small stones stacked one on top of the other or, as my younger son, Carter, exclaimed, ebenezers!

We might be mostly familiar with the word *ebenezer* from Charles Dickens's classic, *A Christmas Carol*. Part of Dickens's brilliance in that book is naming the main character Ebenezer. That word, in Hebrew, means "stone of help." And isn't Ebenezer Scrooge a stone of help?

In the book of 1 Samuel, the prophet Samuel stacks stones on top of each other and calls it an ebenezer—a marker of the hope he had in God. There, in Albuquerque, we saw the same: stones stacked one on top of the other into small monuments. And they were all around us.

Carter got down and started to make his own ebenezer from some loose rocks. Jackson, my older, joined in. When they were done, my wife, Dana, and I asked them what they were remembering with their stones of help, their ebenezers. Carter said, "Papa the Great," what he called Dana's grandfather; a man whom we'd just buried the day before. Jackson said, "Quincy," the name we had picked out for a baby we lost to a miscarriage.

Truly, they understood what it is to erect an ebenezer; a stone of help.

Life for my family these last few months has been marked by reasons to lose hope. As I wrote these pages, I waited for health insurance to approve life-giving medical treatment while suffering with physical ailments like chronic fatigue, unusual and severe aches and pains, unrelenting nausea, and congestion. For the last many months, I suffered greatly in my body, eventually landing me in the hospital in December 2023, with what I called my infection sandwich: two different strains of antibiotic-resistant sinusitis, bronchitis, pneumonia, respiratory syncytial virus, and mononucleosis, all simultaneously. Excellent medical care after I left the hospital resulted in detecting a condition I have had all my life: primary immunodeficiency. My immune system simply does not function well, and is even weaker now than it's ever been before. Life since I left the hospital has felt like the pandemic all over again: I wear a mask wherever I go, I avoid crowds, and I work from home, per my doctor's orders. I am often isolated.

Such suffering in body affects the mind and the spirit. It has been easy to lose hope. I wrestled with my faith, wrestled with my calling as a pastor, wrestled with the church I served; I wrestled, like Jacob before me, mightily with God. And as I write, I am not yet done with my wrestling. I have good days, where I see hope, and I have hard days, where I find myself mostly despairing. The ups and downs of this season of life have left me weary and worn.

Jackson has also suffered mightily. While I was just starting to get out of bed again, he came down with mono. This disease kept him in bed for three months, struggling with severe headaches and the symptoms they created. In the end, we had to unenroll him from school, causing him to start eighth grade all over again through a homeschool program. He misses his friends and the band program he adores. Like me, he has undergone his own emotional and spiritual journey, one he continues to walk.

The rest of the family sojourned with me and Jackson. We have experienced the ups and downs, the wrestling, the despair, the hope, together. God has joined us together, and like a body, what one part feels, every part feels. At times, this reality engenders tremendous support; at other times, all of us suffering simultaneously leaves us weary, worn, and hopeless.

Then, just as we saw light at the end of the tunnel, we all felt like we'd been kicked while we were down. The church I served grew impatient with my recovery and voted to seek a new senior pastor. In The United Methodist Church, this rarely happens; yet, it happened to me. I found myself without a job, suddenly and cruelly. The night after I got the news, Carter was inconsolable, wailing for hours. He spoke for all of us as we each grieved mightily.

Our bouts with illness, the waiting for treatment to begin, and all the questions left us feeling unstable and traumatized, wondering what new crisis life would bring next. The church's decision added significantly to that feeling, ushering us further into the darkness that so often characterizes suffering.

It's fair to say that, for all four of us, these past several months have been the hardest season of our lives. In a four-month period, two of us lost our health, I lost my job, Jackson lost his school, and our lives felt turned upside down. Our suffering was and is great.

What do we do in moments like this? As a family, we ask ourselves that question many times. Dana and I sometimes stare at each other, asking such a question, often without answer. What do any of us do in moments like this, where suffering seems to take hold and not let go? Where we might know in our heads that this will not be forever, but our hearts and souls have yet to realize such wonderful knowledge?

Perhaps you can relate to times of suffering like this, whether in the past or in your present reality. If so, this book is for you. I must confess, it is also for me. Churches I served often comment to me how helpful my sermons and teachings around suffering are. Now, I must turn back to my own teachings, back to the scriptures on which they are based, to rediscover my faith afresh and anew. I invite you along this journey with me, hoping that as I think about how to handle my own suffering, I can help you find the way forward with your suffering.

The still, small, voice of God, suggesting I write this book as a means of therapy, came through a southern drawl on the other end of my phone. One of my dearest friends suggested this project to me after listening to how I have been suffering. Friendships, as I have found, are vital during periods of such suffering. The despair and hardship of suffering lies to us, telling us to isolate, that no one cares, that we best not trouble others with our issues. At times, I believed such lies, only to find my friends and family rally around me yet again, after I am sure I must have exhausted their sympathies.

Friendship is one answer to the question "What do we do in moments like this?" And as I worked on this book, I found several more answers. Some days I cling to a faith that says God will provide, healing and health will prevail, God will use my suffering to God's glory, and that one day, I will look back on this season of life and see how God redeemed my suffering to help others and to make me stronger. One day.

But that day is not today. Nor will it be tomorrow. So what do we, a people of faith, do while we wait for this future? And then, what about when the future seems uncertain, a faraway surety outside of our grasp? At times during my illness, and at times as I watched Jackson suffer, I wondered about our mortality. When we suffer such that death becomes a watchword, looking out from the ramparts of our lives, glimpsing scenes of death coming like a marauding army, what do we, as a people of faith, do?

Throughout this book, I endeavor to answer that question. God made us to be doers. Consider how often scripture admonishes us to be things like "doers, not hearers" of the word (James 1:22). For the majority of our lives, we work, we contribute, we do. When suffering impedes our ability to do, we suffer all the more because we struggle to live out who God made us to be. Our identities, our sense of self, connects deeply with our labor, from laundry to preaching, from financial planning to dishes, from bedtime routines to statistical analyses, from staff supervision to pruning bushes. God made us to do that labor, and God made us to be doers, so when we cannot do what we normally do, what do we do?

It turns out God has given us things to do even when suffering. As I suffer, I find that when I care for others, I experience care myself. Even when I make a pastoral care call and we never talk about me, I yet experience a certain mystical care for myself. Caring for others is one thing I have found to do. I have also, oddly, found joy in pruning. Our yard needs serious attention. As I have energy and need a physical outlet, I prune. Seeing completed work has its own satisfaction, but my mind wanders, as I listen to jazz or the alt rock of my high school years, to how I am pruning my own life. Getting sick and having to take so much time away from the things I did brings into focus what matters and what does not. So, in pruning, I find joy and I hear God speak.

And, I must confess, I have grown rather obsessive about my New York Times crossword scoring. As I write, I am on a ninety-six-day streak of completing the daily crossword, and also realizing with some panic that I have not yet completed today's! Although the hour grows late, I must, because I have found great joy in completing these crosswords. Then, I also complete the mini crossword, the Wordle, and another new word search game because Jackson, Dana, and two of our dearest friends share our scores every day.

Before I got sick, it seemed such a small thing. Now, it feels like everything.

For finding joy, seeking connection, focusing on what truly matters in life, caring for others—these things take on new and urgent importance when we cannot do as we once did. There are still other things we can do, and as we walk the journey of this book together, we will examine all this and more.

My hope, and my prayer, is that this book will be a practical manual for you, whether for your own suffering or as you care for a loved one who is suffering. That's why I have subtitled the book as a field guide through the land of suffering, a land we can rightly characterize as the wilderness. Throughout scripture, the wilderness is the place of chaos, dismay, despair, fear—suffering. We must all walk through the wilderness from time to time, journeying just as Christ did when tempted in the desert and when walking the path to Golgotha.

As we depart on this journey, we look first at how to trust God. This does not presume that we already trust God, nor that we will at the end of the chapter, but it forms a framework to understand all that will come throughout this book. After all, God is good, and yet we are experiencing something other than good. How can we trust that God will provide, prevail, and persevere for us? Parts One through Three cannot make sense without first attending to our relationship with God, whether we currently trust God, are struggling to trust God, or don't trust God at all.

Having looked at our divine-human relationship, this field guide then moves further into the land of suffering by looking at what to expect in Part 1: Getting Acquainted. When we look out at the wilderness, what do we see? And when we have seen, how do we understand? The ancients thought of the wilderness as chaos in part because strange creatures lived there. When we suffer, we encounter all sorts of strange things. How do we understand what we find? How can we make sense of the fact that God allowed this to happen? Did God cause this to happen? Did my own sin cause this to happen? These are the kinds of questions we encounter in the wilderness.

Once oriented to the wilderness of suffering, we then look for strategies for survival in Part 2: Survival Strategies. Like any good field guide, we need to know how to survive in this wilderness, such as hoisting food up a tree to keep it from bears, or relying on friends. When suffering, we need to know what to do now in a very practical sense. How do we survive suffering that can seem overwhelming, a suffering that can seem to threaten to tear down the lives we have built? One of my doctors recently said that my life had been "turned upside down." She is right! Life turned upside down is disorienting. The wilderness is disorienting. How do we survive such disorientation? The bulk of the chapters ahead give us answers to that question, helping us survive.

We focus on the here and now also because, too often, spiritual advice we might hear during suffering focuses on the future. Friends, pastors, and others in our lives, in trying to be helpful, may tell us simply to wait, knowing that God will restore. They may say things like, "God works all things together for good," or "God won't give you more than you can handle." Sometimes, I even quote these things to myself! Such hopes, as I am sure you are aware, quickly die when suffering enters our lives. They die because they are shallow; scripture pulled out of context. Our faith, and indeed God, demands better.

While we journey through the land of suffering, these clichés are insufficient. God has given us tools to handle our suffering now, while we wait. We are empowered, as we will see, to not only survive but even thrive in the land of suffering, finding ourselves refined. We do indeed have hope in the future, for Christ is triumphant. But while we are on the journey through the wilderness, we need to know how to survive so we can reach that moment in the future where we will know, as the old hymn says, victory in Jesus. Otherwise, suffering can seem to threaten to consume, trapping us forever in the wilderness.

Only once we have learned these survival skills do we turn toward hope in the future, the content of Part 3: Discovering Hope. While sojourning in the wilderness, using the tools God has given us, learning to understand what we encounter and survive its challenges, how do we look toward the future with hope? Where do we find hope? These chapters address this crucial question after we have learned to recognize the wilderness, accept our limitations, and discover how God has empowered us to trek through this foreign, weary, and dark land.

After each chapter, you'll see a page dedicated to "Field Notes." This is for your use, to react and process as you read and journey through the land of suffering. I designed this book to be a practical guide, wanting you as the reader to find it not only a helpful guide for today, but hopefully a guide for the future. Each Field Note contains a prompt to address. Feel free to adjust or ignore that prompt as you see fit, recording your response here in this book. These pages are designed for your use, with the prompts merely a guide to begin to react and reflect after reading each chapter.

By the time you reach the conclusion, I pray you have a renewed sense of hope—hope based in knowing how to survive and perhaps even thrive during this time of suffering. I am finding my way, too, and as I write, as I labor on this book, I am finding that God is not only teaching me how to survive, but even how to thrive, for God has empowered me, and you, too, to walk through this land of suffering.

Those ebenezers at the Petroglyphs National Monument stand out in our collective memory as a family. In the middle of what can only be described as a wilderness, even with the orderly city of Albuquerque clearly visible nearby, we raised our stones of help. Perhaps that is the greatest thing we can do in the wilderness: defy the voices in our heads that tell us to despair, tell us to quit, tell us there is no future, by erecting a stone of help—a monument to the God who inspires our faith that the suffering will not have the final word. When we erect such ebenezers, we defiantly say to the forces of suffering, "God's not done with me yet!"

So let us cry with the poet and preacher Robert Robinson, "Here I raise mine ebenezer; hither by thy help I'm come; and I hope, by thy good pleasure, safely to arrive at home … come, thou Fount of every blessing, tune [our] heart[s] to sing thy praise," even in this wilderness.

Field Notes

Describe the suffering you know today. What led you to read this book? What do you hope to gain? Perhaps put your answers in a written prayer to God.

Chapter 2

How to Trust God

Protect me, O God, for in you I take refuge.
I say to the Lord, "You are my Lord;
I have no good apart from you."
As for the holy ones in the land, they are the noble ones
in whom is all my delight.
Those who choose another god multiply their sorrows;
their drink offerings of blood I will not pour out
or take their names upon my lips.
The Lord is my chosen portion and my cup;
you hold my lot.
The boundary lines have fallen for me in pleasant places;
I have a goodly heritage.
I bless the Lord, who gives me counsel;
in the night also my heart instructs me.
I keep the Lord always before me;
because he is at my right hand, I shall not be moved.
Therefore my heart is glad, and my soul rejoices;
my body also rests secure.
For you do not give me up to Sheol
or let your faithful one see the Pit.
You show me the path of life.
In your presence there is fullness of joy;
in your right hand are pleasures forevermore.
—Psalm 16

WE HAD GREAT NEIGHBORS when we first lived in Macon, Georgia. The kind of neighbors that become deep, lifelong friends. The kind of neighbors where we just walked into one another's homes without knocking. In fact, those neighbors remain dear friends today. And back when we lived on Highland Terrace together, we spent much time on one another's front porches.

Such was the day that I walked over to sit on our friends' porch after a long day of working on seminary papers and assignments. On the porch was a friend of our neighbors'. As we got introduced, she asked the classic question, "What do you do?" Now, if you're a pastor, that's a loaded question. I've had all sorts of reactions to telling people I'm a pastor, many of them negative. But this one took the cake. She looked at me and said, with some choice words interspersed throughout, "How do you believe that [stuff]?"

I was taken aback, but I wasn't offended. I was empathic. It's the classic question of faith. How do we believe what we proclaim to believe? How do we believe what the creeds say? How do we believe that stuff?

One can imagine David, to whom this psalm is ascribed, getting asked, "How do you believe that stuff?" The mighty ones, the holy ones, the noble ones that he refers to are a people he knows, he has relationship with, and they're worshipping pagan gods. They do not believe what David declares: that the boundary lines have fallen for him in pleasant places, that he has a peaceful heart and a secure body because God has given him the path of life, that in God's presence he finds joy and pleasures forevermore.

Which are funny things for David to say, considering that at this point in his life, he's being chased by the current king of Israel, Saul, and the king's army; hiding in caves; utterly rejected by most people. His life is anything but pleasant. And, it's God who got him into this mess! He was a simple shepherd until God decided to raise him up to defeat Goliath. And then, he could have just remained a folk hero, but God had to go and anoint him king of Israel while Israel already had a king!

David declares his faith, his trust, in God over and against his lived experience and his friends' beliefs. How could he believe that stuff?

It's a relevant question for today. Many people are asking anyone of faith, regardless of tradition, how they can believe that stuff. The fastest growing segment of religion are those who hold to no belief system, whether "spiritual but not religious" or simply rejecting spirituality in total. So it's fair to say if we're not getting asked directly how we believe what we confess, many around us are asking that question silently. If someone asked you, "How do you believe that stuff," how would you respond?

Perhaps, mindful of suffering, it's hard to answer that question ourselves. Doubt settles in, making us ask again, "How do I believe this stuff?" That is OK—doubt is the fertile soil in which faith grows. As we begin this journey through the land of suffering, we may find ourselves asking, wondering, how do we believe this stuff?

Way back in the day, bishops of the church asked themselves this same question. They answered it, and we call their answer the Nicene Creed. I remember learning about it for the first time in seminary, thinking that this was the most verbose and odd creed I'd ever heard. We were deep in the weeds of learning about the debates that gave rise to the Council of Nicaea, the one that gave us our Bibles as they are today and the one that developed this creed. There were massive debates about a variety of issues, especially revolving around the humanity and divinity of Christ. They were asking themselves, "How do we believe this stuff about Jesus?"

Santa Claus helped them answer that question. As the debates raged, two sides formed. On the one side was St. Nicholas, one of the primary historical figures that has given rise to our modern conception of Santa Claus. That's because St. Nicholas was known for taking bags of money and leaving them at the homes of the poor under the cover of darkness, sort of like Santa Claus delivering presents on the night of Christmas Eve. Here at Nicaea, just south of Constantinople, or what's known today as Istanbul, St. Nicholas was arguing that Jesus was of the same stuff, or of the same being, as the Father;

in Greek, the word *homoousious*. Arius, on the other hand, showed up ready to argue that Jesus was of similar stuff to the Father, but not the same; of similar being but not the same being. The Greek word for that is *homoiousious*. Yes, there's one letter difference between the two words; the letter "I" inserted before -ousious. They were arguing, at a certain level, over one letter in a word.

Today, that might seem kind of ridiculous, but the argument became so heated between the two sides that, as Arius was speaking, St. Nicholas—Santa Claus, remember—crossed the room and slapped Arius across the face. Bishops from everywhere quickly pulled the two men apart before they could get into a brawl. It might be good to tell your children and grandchildren this Christmas that they'd better not make Santa angry by believing heretical things!

But Arius, St. Nicholas, and all the bishops gathered in Nicaea wanted to know: How do we believe this stuff?

How does David believe this stuff?

How do we believe this stuff?

At the base of that question is a question of trust: How do we trust that God is who we proclaim God to be?

This is one of the things creeds do for us. They state at a base level what we believe to be true about God. We believe that God is one in three, Father, Son, and Holy Spirit. We believe that through God all things were created and that each of the members of the Trinity have a role to play in that creation.

We believe many things about Jesus, as evidenced in the paragraph about him in the Nicene Creed: that he was and is God, made flesh, but still God; that Jesus came in human form for our sake, to suffer death and be buried, to rise again in accordance with the scriptures and to be seated at the right hand of the Father, where he waits to come again.

We then say we believe in the Holy Spirit, who proceeds from the Father and the Son; that we believe in the holy catholic and apostolic church; in other words, in a church that is universal and run by disciples in a hierarchy whose head are bishops.

We have many things to say in our creeds, but they are the bedrock, the foundation, of our faith. They are, as David would say in Psalm 16, the boundary lines for us as a faith, which we might agree with David and say they have fallen for us in pleasant places. The creed states our answer to the question, "Who is God? What do you believe?"

But note with me that's not the question we're asking. We're not wondering what we believe, which is what the creeds state. No, we're asking, "How do we believe this stuff?" In other words, how do we trust that what the creed says is true?

Trust is a function of character and competence.[1] Consider people in your lives whom you trust. We trust them because they are who they say they are and because they do what they say they'll do. Whenever I start at a new church, building trust is job Number 1. I recognize that anything we do together, any ways that we might respond to the movement of the Holy Spirit among us, requires that the church trust me and my leadership. That means that church trusts that I am who I say I am, that I act in ways that are congruent with what I proclaim, and that I do what I say I will do, that I have follow through; in other words, trusting my character and competence.

This is Stephen M. R. Covey's definition of trust in his classic book on leadership, *The Speed of Trust*. He notes that where trust is present, organizations move quickly to make decisions, to take risks, and move in the same direction, to the great benefit of that organization and those whom they serve. But where trust is not present or is threatened, the organization's ability to move and make decisions and take risks slows down and sometimes stops completely, not only doing a great disservice to those they serve, but also threatening the very foundation of the organization itself. Where character and competence cannot be trusted, relationships fall apart and organizations break down.

Consider the story behind the phrase "and from the Son" in the Nicene Creed, a phrase known as the filioque. In the original form after the Council of Nicaea, the creed says "We believe in the Holy

Spirit ... who proceeds from the Father." The Council of Toledo in the year 589 added the filioque, the phrase, "and from the Son," to say that Holy Spirit proceeds both from the Father and the Son. But some didn't like the addition of the filioque. They felt like no one could change the creed from Nicaea, set back in the year 325.

The debate over those four words, "and from the Son," came to a boil in the year 1054. That year, Pope Leo IX excommunicated the bishop of Constantinople, Michael Cerularius, for several things, including his unwillingness to adopt the filioque. Michael Cerularius, thinking he was more powerful than the pope, excommunicated Leo IX. From this moment of dueling excommunications, the church in the west, headed by Rome, and the church in the east, headed by Constantinople, broke apart from one another. This is one of the reasons why, today, we have Catholic churches and Orthodox churches: The filioque controversy split the church into Catholic and Orthodox sects. In fact, those dueling excommunications stood as in effect until 1965, when Pope Paul VI and his counterpart in the Orthodox Church, Athenagoras I, cancelled the excommunications issued by their forebears 1,011 years prior. When we say, "and from the Son," in the Nicene Creed, behind those four words is a powerful story of the effect of distrust within the church and, for that matter, the effect of distrust in any organization or relationship.

This incident that led to division, a breakdown of the organization of the church and a loss of relationships, just as Covey describes, came down to questions of character and competence. Could Leo IX trust that Michael Cerularius was who he said he was if he wouldn't believe in the filioque? Apparently not. Leo did not trust the character of his counterpart. Could Michael Cerularius trust that Leo IX actually had the power to excommunicate him? Apparently not. He could not trust the competence of his counterpart.

Trust is a function of character and competence.

And so it is with God.

David's answer to "How do you believe that stuff" would be to say he had seen God prove to have good character and be competent over and over again in his life. The boundary lines have fallen in pleasant places. He has a goodly inheritance, as he says in the Psalm, because God has provided, fulfilling promises, just as God said he would. That's competence that can be trusted.

And in verse 7, we see David confessing that God is who God says he is: at night, God gives him counsel. God said, "Never will I leave you nor forsake you" and has indeed remained present with David. God said he would be David's God. God said he had a plan and is more powerful than Saul and any of the gods his contemporaries are worshipping. And in David's life, he's seen God prove all this to be true. That's character that can be trusted.

Psalm 16 functions like a creed. It's a basic statement of belief, here by David; a basic statement of trust that God is who God says he is and that God will do what God says he would do; that God can be trusted because God's character and competence are trustworthy.

That's what our creeds do. They declare who God is, sometimes with funky language like in the Nicene Creed, but they state this is what we believe about who God is. We believe that God is one in three, we believe that Jesus Christ came for us, and we believe that the Holy Spirit lives within us and energizes our holy, catholic, and apostolic church. We believe that God is for us, seen in providing Jesus Christ. We believe that God's character can be trusted.

And the creed also tells us that God's competence can be trusted. Consider the end of the creed: "We acknowledge one baptism for the forgiveness of sins. We look for the resurrection of the dead and the life of the world to come." We believe that God will do what God said he would do: forgive our sins and raise us to new life, both in this life and the next.

And then, in the creed, we declare that if God took care of Jesus "for our sake," as the creed said, God will take care of us. In the creed, we claim that we trust that God will do what God said he would do; that God is competent.

So how do we believe that stuff? The only way to answer that question really is to say we trust God. We believe God is who God says he is and that God will do what God said he would do; we trust God's character and competence.

In the midst of suffering, believing we can trust God takes on additional importance. At times, we will doubt while journeying through the land of suffering. Such doubt is OK and to be expected. But if we will consider God's character and competence while on this journey, while experiencing doubt, we will find our way again to trusting God.

It's thus that we begin here, before looking at the nature of suffering itself and talking about strategies for finding our way through the land of suffering. Before we embark on the journey, we must consider trust in God. Times of suffering often hurt our trust, what we might refer to as our faith. We wonder about God's character when asking, "Why would a good God allow this to happen?" We wonder about God's competence when asking, "Why hasn't God fixed this already?" Going into reading this book, I would expect that you bring questions of trust into the conversation. That is fine and to be expected!

In thinking about trust as a function of character and competence, we give ourselves a framework for building trust, whether regaining trust in God or strengthening the trust we already have. As we go through the chapters, allow yourself to question God, to confront God even, while maintaining an open mind to what God can do. Chapters ahead will ask you to consider the past, looking back to where God has been faithful before. No matter how you feel about God today, look back to that past with an open mind and keep open the possibility that God can be trusted again.

For me, on that porch that day when I got asked, "How do you believe that stuff," my first answer was some humor. I told her that, first, I don't believe it's "stuff," using the word that she had actually used to describe faith. Then I said I had made a conscious choice based out of my experience. I had questioned God for a time. Based on my experiences before, I did not feel that God was who he said he is and I felt that God could not be trusted to do what God said he would do. I did not trust the character and competence of God. My experience of God after we moved back to Macon—finding healing in the church we attended, experiencing the power of God's presence in my life personally, finding powerful support in the community around us at the church—led me to a place where I could trust God's character and competence. And so, I made a choice and joined the church, professing that I believed; that I trusted.

So it is with the life of faith, especially in times of suffering. We all go through times of trust and distrust in God's character and competence. Faith asks us to believe that God can be trusted again, keeping an open mind and heart to what God will do. As you read, I hope that not only will you find practical advice for the journey through the land of suffering, but also further reasons to trust the character and competence of God.

At the base of how we believe is trust.

The Nicene Creed has stories behind it: stories of a violent Santa Claus. Stories of dueling excommunications. Stories of humanity trying to figure out who God is and how to relate to God. Stories of learning to trust in God's character and competence. Stories, ultimately, seeking to answer that question, "How do you believe that stuff?"

And isn't that our story?

Field Notes

As you look ahead to these chapters, where do you trust God's character and competence? Where is that trust challenged? Be real with yourself and God, helping open your heart to what God will do through succeeding chapters.

Part 1

Getting Acquainted

*In the bleak midwinter, frosty wind made moan,
earth stood hard as iron, water like a stone;
snow had fallen, snow on snow, snow on snow,
in the bleak midwinter, long ago.*

*Our God, heaven cannot hold him, nor earth sustain;
heaven and earth shall flee away when he comes to reign.
In the bleak midwinter a stable place sufficed
the Lord God Almighty, Jesus Christ.*

*Enough for him, whom cherubim worship night and day,
Breastful of milk, and a mangerful of hay:
Enough for him, whom angels fall before,
The ox and ass and camel which adore.*

*Angels and archangels may have gathered there,
cherubim and seraphim thronged the air;
but his mother only, in her maiden bliss,
worshipped the beloved with a kiss.*

*What can I give him, poor as I am?
If I were a shepherd, I would bring a lamb;
if I were a Wise Man I would do my part;
yet what I can I give him: give him my heart.*

—Christina G. Rossetti, 1872

CHAPTER 3

Expect Hardship

"Then they will hand you over to be tortured and will put you to death, and you will be hated by all nations because of my name. Then many will fall away, and they will betray one another and hate one another. And many false prophets will arise and lead many astray. And because of the increase of lawlessness, the love of many will grow cold. But the one who endures to the end will be saved. And this good news of the kingdom will be proclaimed throughout the world, as a testimony to all the nations, and then the end will come."—Matthew 24:9-14

As much as we know suffering brings hardship, we yet struggle to accept it. This struggle has certainly been true for me. As I suffer, encountering various challenges, often I find myself wrestling with the hardship brought by those challenges. Then when I move through and accept the hardship, I wonder why I wrestled in the first place. Why couldn't I simply accept the hardship?

Together, we embark on this first leg of the journey in these next several chapters, learning what to expect and looking first at hardship. As we begin, I invite you to pour a favorite drink, get comfortable and cozy, and consider the exact opposite: winter.

We know when winter is coming. Temperatures fall and leaves change colors; we can all feel instinctually the changing of the seasons.

And when we feel those changes, we bundle up with our jackets and face the cold winter wind.

Every year we know when winter is coming.

I personally love winter, but even I cannot deny that winter is a time of foreboding, a stark time of grays and whites and signs of decay and even death—the world awaiting renewal. The idea that winter is coming hits home on a spiritual level as it refers to the coming of challenge, difficulty, and suffering. Things like the dark night of our soul, the season of discontent, the deepest valley, times of suffering.

Winter is coming.

So says Jesus in this little apocalypse, a section of the Gospel of Matthew.

There, Jesus makes no bones about it: winter comes, storms rage, nations totter, and disaster strikes. Jesus mentions these things to tell us they're normal, they're part of living life on this planet, and they're to be expected. These are external problems, external difficulties, things out in the world that sometimes affect us.

Beginning in verse 9, Jesus then shifts to inward things, personal suffering: betrayal, hatred, torture, ridicule, setbacks, and even death. In our lives, we've also known personal suffering. We've known dark nights of our souls, seasons of discontent, the deepest and darkest valleys, times of suffering. We've known family divisions, disputes, and the loss of relationships. We've known betrayal, just like Jesus mentions here, of those supposedly closest to us or those who we thought cared for us. We've known the particular kind of torture that is being the subject of gossip. We've known what it is to be hated by others for what we've done or said. We've known financial downturns. We've known shattering medical diagnoses. We've known times of despair because of tragedy.

We've known winter.

Winter isn't coming. It's been here. It's stayed a while. Maybe you're living in a winter in your life right now: a dark night of your soul, a season of discontent, a deepest valley, a time of suffering.

Jesus says to expect this. Jesus says this is normal. Jesus says this is how the world works. Jesus says there will be suffering because of wars, natural disasters, people fighting, and personal tragedies. Jesus says suffering, even personal suffering, has happened, is happening, and will continue to happen.

Jesus says this is good news.

That doesn't feel right. That doesn't feel good. That feels contradictory at best and insensitive at worst. But there, at the start of verse 14, Jesus says this is good news: "And this good news of the kingdom will be proclaimed throughout the world" (Matthew 24:14).

How in the world is this good news? How is it good news that winter is coming, especially knowing that it might stay for quite a while? How is it good news to know suffering is coming?

Imagine this scene with me: Jesus, sitting near the temple in Jerusalem with his disciples. They've asked him about the end times. He's pointing to the temple complex, the most sacred site of their faith, the place where God was understood to literally dwell, and saying it's all going to be destroyed. Life as they know it is about to change forever.

But he's not just talking about the temple being destroyed. He's also talking about the remainder of that week, a week we call today Holy Week.

Jesus will endure all the travesties of verses 9-11: betrayal, torture, hatred, false accusations and prophets leading people away from him, and finally death on a cross. For Jesus, winter is coming. And quickly approaching. He knows what's coming. He knows what he's about to endure. He knows the chaos of the world will soon catch up to him.

So he says to himself as much as to the disciples, he says to himself as much as he says to us today, that the facing of death, the coming of torture, betrayal, and suffering, is the "good news of the kingdom ... " (Matthew 24:14).

How is this good news?

Clearly, Jesus knows what it is to suffer. He saw what was headed his way through this Holy Week.

But even for him, how is that good news?

Let's be clear: We're not wrong to ask that question. When suffering, bad news feels devastating and even good news can feel dull.

Consider the day I received news that we would be receiving a generous reimbursement of our medical bills, which had totaled $15,000 over six months. On that same day, I also received news that lab results I needed for insurance approval of treatment for my primary immunodeficiency would take twelve to fourteen days, rather than one to two days, to get back. The bad news about my labs dominated my thoughts and mood, leaving me feeling sour and irritable, even though I had also received astoundingly good news just hours before!

Suffering does that. The hardship we can expect skews our perceptions and understandings, making bad news seem worse than it is and good news less so. When hearing that suffering, expected hardship, is good news, we might not only wonder how Jesus can say that but react with anger. How could Jesus say such a thing? Where's the empathy we need? It's as if we have broken our leg and a friend tells us they just broke a personal record running. Jesus declaring suffering to be good news feels insensitive.

When we're suffering, experiencing hardship, we see the bad before the good. When Jesus discusses how he is about to suffer, he's talking about what we call Maundy Thursday and Good Friday. He clearly sees the bad coming his way. But Jesus's perception doesn't end on Friday. And as Christians, neither should ours.

Our faith carries us through Friday to Sunday, Easter Sunday.

Winter is coming. But so is resurrection.

Like the trees and grass of the field in spring, new life blooms where old life had died. Like the light shining into the dark valley, like the kindness of our church and community when we suffer, like the morning after a long night, new life breaks in where once there was death.

That's the good news of the kingdom. "And this good news of the kingdom [that resurrection is coming], will be proclaimed throughout the world, as a testimony to all the nations … " (Matthew 24:14).

Winter is coming. But so is resurrection.

We will suffer. Jesus makes that abundantly clear. Humanity is prone to suffering. In fact, Christians will know more suffering in this life than others because we carry the name of Christ into a broken world. It's another way Jesus points to this fact: Religion doesn't make our lives easier. It doesn't lead us to avoid suffering. It doesn't take away suffering or prevent suffering. There are many books saying otherwise. They sell a snake oil faith. To follow Jesus is to take up our cross, bearing its burden.

When we reject such Pollyanna religion, we find faith does make life better because it teaches us how to find the light in the dark night of our soul, how to find contentment during a season of discontentment, how to walk up the mountain out of the deepest valley, how to witness when the world tells us we're fools, how to walk into the suffering of others, shining the light of Christ, even though it makes us suffer, and how to boldly walk into our own suffering, facing it head on. In sum, it teaches us how to hold on to hope during winter, because we know deep in our souls: Resurrection is coming.

We live in a cycle—one we might like to avoid, but one that will come upon us whether we want it to or not. We go through seasons of winter, of suffering, into seasons of spring, of resurrection. These come and go, but for those who are in Christ, no matter how deep and dark the winter, resurrection will always come. And that is, indeed, good news.

The challenge before us—you, dear reader, and me—is to walk headlong into our suffering. When suffering comes, it's tempting to try to avoid it, deny it, bargain with it, get angry about it. All those things are normal human reactions; in fact, they're some of the stages of grief. Grief sets in whenever our hearts and minds have to adapt to a new reality that doesn't look at all like our hopes and dreams. And that's always challenging, always difficult, always a winter season in our lives.

The only way to get through it, to walk up the mountain from the valley, to wake up to a new morning after the dark night of our soul, is to walk headlong into the suffering—to embrace winter. Embrace the suffering. Know the suffering. Bundle up and live into the winter season.

Winter has come. But we have confidence as we brace and face the cold, cruel, wind of suffering: Resurrection is coming.

There's a great old jazz standard that speaks directly to this. After wrestling, tossing and turning, with suffering in her life, the singer invites her heartache to sit down at the table of her heart. Rather than continue to wrestle, she accepts and admits that the heartache, this suffering she knows, will be hanging around for a while. In a later rendition, another singer improves, inviting the heartache to not only sit down at the table but get comfortable.

I appreciate this song so much because the singer embraces suffering and models for us what we are to do. She's done denying; she's done avoiding. She's walked headlong into her personal winter.

We must do the same.

Acceptance, inviting our suffering to pull up a chair to the table of our hearts, also makes room at the table for healing. But let us note that the song misses a crucial fact: Resurrection is coming. The heartache might pull up a chair for a while, but it's not forever. The financial downturn might be devastating, but it's not forever. The betrayal might sting like a hundred bees, but it's not forever. The loss and grief might shroud us with its darkness like an invisible blanket, but it's not forever. The ridicule we endure because we witness to our faith might isolate us in loneliness, but it's not forever. The hatred we experience because we stand up against the false prophets of end times predictions, conspiracy theories, and the like might wound us like a knife to the heart, but it's not forever.

It's not forever because in those winters we know that resurrection is coming.

And even when our suffering brings with it the shadow of death, we know with sure and certain hope that even death is not the end for us. We will be resurrected and our hearts at their true home with Christ. And, perhaps most importantly, those we leave behind will also know resurrection power in the midst of their grief. Even in death, resurrection is coming.

So we can look forward with hope, we can be in the midst of our present suffering with hope, we can sit in the darkness with hope, we can invite heartache, depression, cancer, death, despair, hatred, betrayal, to pull up a chair for a while and get comfortable because we know this good news of the kingdom: Resurrection is coming.

In the land of suffering, we should expect hardship. It comes with the territory. But the call of the kingdom is to hard work. Taking up our cross daily is hard work. Winter is hard work. The world gives us winters. God gives us resurrections.

Perhaps Christina Rossetti, the English poet, put it best. We typically hear her poem as a hymn of the same name at Advent, but I think her words speak to any winter season of life. She says in the first and final verses, "In the bleak midwinter, frosty wind made moan, earth stood hard as iron, water like a stone; snow had fallen, snow on snow, snow on snow, in the bleak midwinter, long ago … . What can I give him, poor as I am? If I were a shepherd, I would bring a lamb; if I were a Wise Man, I would do my part; yet what I can I give him: give him my heart."[2]

In the bleak midwinter seasons of life, we should expect hardship. That hardship can seem to overwhelm, but there's yet good news. Into such a season was Jesus born, and through his own time of hardship, he revealed God's resurrection power. The hardship doesn't have the final word. But we must accept the current season of suffering. Invite the suffering to pull up a chair to the table of your heart.

And then, with Christina Rossetti, give Jesus your heart.

Field Notes

What suffering do you need to invite to the table of your heart? How can you both embrace your suffering and the notion that resurrection is coming?

Chapter 4

Expect Change

"When [Jesus] had come near Bethphage and Bethany, at the place called the Mount of Olives, he sent two of the disciples saying, 'Go into the village ahead of you, and as you enter it you will find tied there a colt that has never been ridden. Untie it and bring it here. If anyone asks you, 'Why are you untying it?' just say this, 'the Lord needs it.' So those who were sent departed and found it as he had told them. As they were untying the colt, its owners asked them, 'Why are you untying the colt?' They said, 'The Lord needs it.' Then they brought it to Jesus, and after throwing their cloaks on the colt, they set Jesus on it. As he rode along, people kept spreading their cloaks on the road. Now as he was approaching the path down the Mount of Olives, the whole multitude of the disciples began to praise God joyfully with a loud voice for all the deeds of power that they had seen, saying, 'Blessed is the king who comes in the name of the Lord! Peace in heaven, and glory in the highest heaven!' Some of the Pharisees in the crowd said to him, 'Teacher, order your disciples to stop.' He answered, 'I tell you, if these were silent, the stones would shout out.'"
—Luke 19:29-40

IN THE LAND OF SUFFERING, we expect to encounter hardship—the midwinter seasons of life. As we encounter and experience that hardship, we also experience tremendous change. Of course, we have heard the old maxims like "the only constant is change," but change seems harder, crueler perhaps, when we suffer. But when we know to expect change, it becomes easier to accept.

Certainly, Jesus knew about change. Imagine how he must have felt riding into Jerusalem on that first Palm Sunday. Think back to Palm Sundays you have known. I imagine my children walking down the aisle of churches I served, waving palm branches. The sanctuary looks so green with palm arrangements, people holding fronds, and sometimes, wearing crosses made of palms pinned to dresses and lapels. Palm Sunday has so much joy to it, so much pomp and circumstance.

But Palm Sunday also foretells a great change coming. Indeed, everything in Luke's gospel has been moving toward this moment. The gospel begins with the ends of the earth, then moves to the greater region of the Middle East, then to Judea and Samaria, and then finally centers in Jerusalem, beginning with this Palm Sunday moment where Jesus arrives in triumphant procession. Luke does this quite on purpose; in Acts, he reverses the direction, starting in Jerusalem and then moving into Judea, Samaria, and the rest of the world by the end of that book. It's a brilliant literary device!

As he rides into Jerusalem, Jesus upstages the Roman rulers, especially Pilate, who likes to ride in through a triumphant parade at this time of year. Jesus is showing that he's the real king, but on a humble colt, not a great stallion, and not with a red carpet but with the humble coats of the everyday person.

And here, in Luke, it's not great masses of people who meet Jesus but rather his disciples. Even so, the pharisees can't take it. They're so worried about what this will mean for their power, because Jesus also means to upstage them and show how their power is built on a sandy foundation.

The politics, the showmanship, the poetry of this moment are great. There are issues of cosmic significance! Especially around power: that earthly power, no matter how grand and great it may be, is nothing compared to God's power. Jesus speaks to this when saying, at the very end, that if the disciples were silent the stones themselves would shout out. Jesus shows and states that true power, the kind of power that can really make a difference, is power characterized by humility, gentleness, and devotion to God.

But there's more to this story than a message about power.

Thursday is coming, with the darkness settling over Jesus and his disciples. Thursday is coming when Judas will betray him. Thursday is coming when he will break the bread and hold up the wine and declare his own death. Thursday is coming when he will go to the garden and be abandoned by his disciples. Thursday is coming when he will be arrested.

And then, Friday is also coming. Friday, when he will stand trial not once but twice. The law, rightly administered, will fail him, both religious and civil law. Friday is coming, when he will walk down the Via Dolorosa. Friday is coming, when he will be nailed to the cross. Friday is coming, when he will cry out, "My God, My God, why have you forsaken me!" (Mark 15:34). Friday is coming, when he will die.

Thursday is coming. Friday is coming. And Jesus knows it, just as we saw in the previous chapter as he forecasts through the little apocalypse.

Imagine the scene: Here he is on this first Palm Sunday, riding in triumphantly on the colt, his disciples cheering him, throwing their coats on the ground as a sign of royalty, just like they did for former kings of Israel. Everything is going very well. His first time in Jerusalem is a smashing success.

But as he rides the colt through the parade, like a hero returning to the United States to ride through New York City, ticker tape falling, as he does that he knows Thursday is coming, Friday is coming, change is coming. That must produce some serious anxiety.

In the last chapter, we alluded to this same scene, of Jesus looking ahead toward these terrible days. But there, in Matthew's little apocalypse, Jesus speaks of these things matter of factly. I have often found myself first thinking of Jesus as resolute, going through such suffering and hardship, such change, without doubt or emotion. Perhaps that describes your image of Jesus, too. Such an image, however, prizes the divinity of Jesus and denies his humanity. Jesus suffered, too, and he must have experienced anxiety about the change headed his way. On Thursday, he'll pray and ask God to take it all away. On Friday, he'll cry out in agony to God from the cross. He knows it's coming.

Like we who await the results of a medical test to confirm what we already know: that we have cancer or some other dreaded disease. Or await the results of a legal case to confirm what we already know: that we're about to lose assets or the dissolution of our marriage. Or await the results at our workplaces to confirm what we already know: that we're losing our job. Those things get perhaps closer to what Jesus is anticipating, the change he knows he will experience, as he rides into Jerusalem.

Thursday is coming. Friday is coming. Change is coming. So it's reasonable, in fact it's essential, to recognize that Jesus must be very anxious about this coming change as he rides into Jerusalem.

And you and I, dear reader, can relate to that anxiety in the ways we all experience change. Suffering produces change, for to suffer means some unforeseen, unwelcome change has come into our lives, upending the previous order. That change begets more change.

For me, change started with coming down with COVID in September 2023. That led to persistent sickness, which eventually landed me in the hospital in December. All through the fall, change came. And when I thought at moments, like in mid-October and early November, that I had conquered the illness and could move on, it would come back, worse than before. The ups and downs, another way of describing all the change I experienced, created anxiety, fear, anger, and a host of other emotions.

Sometimes, change comes because of things that just happen, like falling ill. Sometimes, change happens because of actions we take that we later regret, like a lie or a harsh word. And sometimes, change happens because of actions someone else takes, like when the church committee voted me out, having lost patience with my recovery. Change comes in a variety of ways, leaving us reeling, going through the stages of grief. In fact, no matter how the change comes, we will bargain, deny, get depressed, and find ourselves angry. In the wake of the church's decision, I wrestled long and hard with bouts of depression that would give way to righteous indignation. Change brings us through grief, as we struggle to accommodate to the loss of the previous reality we knew; the former stability.

Such a response is perfectly normal and to be expected, just like Jesus riding into Jerusalem anticipating, anxiously and fearfully, the coming days as he will be maligned, tortured, crucified, and buried.

We know what it's like to expect and anxiously await change. We know what it is to experience change born of suffering. Jesus knows that, too; he experienced it on this Palm Sunday and that first Holy Week.

Change is inevitable. And when we're experiencing anxiety, when we're fearful about or because of change, when we're tossing and turning and up late at night, when we're fighting against a fear that won't let go because of change we expect is coming, how do we handle change?

To answer that question, let's look more closely at this moment of triumphal entry to Jerusalem.

Note that Jesus keeps moving forward. Jesus could have turned his back on Jerusalem, but he didn't. He could have tried to flee the change, but he didn't. He rides headlong into the change, even as it produces anxiety and fear. Doesn't that ring true to our experience? When we're facing change, especially change we didn't ask for and don't want, it's very tempting to try to flee from it, to try to escape it. Of course we can't, but it's a natural reaction. It's reasonable to think that Jesus felt the same impulse, but even if he did, he didn't flee. He kept moving forward, straight into a future he knew was full of change and hardship.

This is the wisdom of that jazz standard from chapter 3. When we invite suffering to take a seat at the table of our hearts, when we embrace it, we accept the change. We must, because otherwise we wrestle fruitlessly, expending energy and stamina we need to make it through our journey in the land of suffering.

So we should also invite change to have a seat at the table of our hearts. Times of suffering naturally evoke fear. That fear says to us that we should avoid change, try to make things the way they once were or, at least, preserve ourselves as we are. The instinct for self-preservation kicks in. Such is a survivalist instinct. Yet, when it comes to suffering, it actually does us harm.

Suffering comes because change has come. Something disrupts the status quo and we struggle to make sense of it, to accept it, to reorient our lives to it. When the church I served voted to seek a new senior pastor, saying they had lost patience with my recovery from primary immunodeficiency, I experienced fear. What would I do for salary after they stopped paying me? Would this require a move from a home we have only owned for two years, from dear friends we have nearby, from a school where my family is so very happy?

As I write, I do not have answers to those questions. I do know, however, that the instinct of fear, born of this sudden change, is to try and preserve things as much as possible. But there is no going back. I cannot return to the church I served even if they wanted me; too much harm has been done. I cannot go and seek my own church in the area; there are no opportunities. Even if there were, in our system the bishop appoints us to churches. It felt as though many doors were closing around us simultaneously.

So, prayerfully and as a family, we determined to open ourselves up wide to see where God would lead. We have embraced the change, understanding that it may yet bring additional hardship, but also understanding that God is sovereign through the change and will provide as we move forward. Our duty is to follow where that change leads.

Some days, I have to again invite the change to have a seat at the table of my heart. Change is not a nice dinner guest; change requires accommodation. But to open myself up, to move boldly into a future I do not understand, is the call of the moment. And that's what I see Jesus doing as he rides into Jerusalem. He rides boldly forward, into a future he knows is fraught and full of hardship, knowing the change will bring grave new realities. Yet he keeps going forward.

In following the example of Jesus from this triumphal entry into Jerusalem, we find the path forward through suffering. There's a mystical reality there: that in choosing to move forward in faith, inviting change to have a seat at the table of our hearts, God gives us what we need for the journey.

God prepared Jesus on that Palm Sunday for all that was ahead. Jesus must have known the same host of emotions we know when anticipating and experiencing change. But he kept moving forward, kept helping, kept leading. So it is for us.

The land of suffering will bring tremendous change. God is faithful through it, and we find our way by moving forward, headlong, into it.

Field Notes

How might you be wrestling with change today? What can you do to move forward into the change suffering has wrought?

Chapter 5

Expect to Lose Security

*"I will extol you, O Lord, for you have drawn me up
and did not let my foes rejoice over me.
O Lord my God, I cried to you for help,
and you have healed me.
O Lord, you brought up my soul from Sheol,
restored me to life from among those gone down to the Pit.
Sing praises to the Lord, O you his faithful ones,
and give thanks to his holy name.
For his anger is but for a moment; his favor is for a lifetime.
Weeping may linger for the night, but joy comes with the morning.
As for me, I said in my prosperity, 'I shall never be moved.'
By your favor, O Lord,
you had established me as a strong mountain;
you hid your face; I was dismayed.
To you, O Lord, I cried,
and to the Lord I made supplication:
'What profit is there in my death, if I go down to the Pit?
Will the dust praise you? Will it tell of your faithfulness?
Hear, O Lord, and be gracious to me! O Lord, be my helper!'
You have turned my mourning into dancing;
you have taken off my sackcloth and clothed me with joy,
so that my soul may praise you and not be silent.
O Lord my God, I will give thanks to you forever."
—Psalm 30*

PERHAPS THE GREATEST CHANGE we experience when suffering is a loss of security, a particular form of change. Such a loss of security brings tremendous hardship. I feel that as I trek through my current suffering journey. At times, I worry about our financial security, with medical bills piling up and when I lost my job. I also worry about our security as a family. And I have had occasions to face my mortality and my son's, feeling insecure in my own health, my own body. Such experiences are tremendous, unsettling change.

How do we create security for ourselves?

For starters, we do lots of things. I imagine many of you are just like me:

I have a savings account. I have investments to pay for Jackson and Carter to go to college. I have a pension. Dana has a pension. We have retirement savings on top of that. We have plans to protect our future.

I also have life insurance, just in case something were to happen to any of the four of us. We have disability policies on the both of us. The United Methodist Church provides great protection for pastors from a variety of troublesome things that happen in life, including disability insurance. Finally, I have homeowner's insurance, car insurance, and an umbrella policy to cover any additional liability we might encounter.

I also make a habit of watching my diet and exercise because I see the benefits it reaps for me today, and I see in those older than me the benefits of lifelong exercise and good eating habits. While recovering, I have doubled down on these, seeing in great relief how these practices help my body grow stronger.

In sum, I'm protecting myself, and my family, against financial downturns, against entering retirement without enough money, against death and disaster, and against health maladies. I'm creating security for myself, my family, and our future. And doing those kinds of things is how we create security for ourselves.

For these are all wise things. And my guess is many of you are doing, or have done, many of the same things or, if you haven't, you're reminding yourself right now to go and do those things. Whether we've begun or not, we create security for ourselves by purchasing insurances of various kinds, saving our money, and choosing healthy habits.

And in those actions, we feel secure. At least, we feel secure until suffering comes. As you know from reading, all of these good, responsible actions couldn't prevent the loss of health, job, and stability in life that our family currently knows.

David also feels secure. He says in Psalm 30:6, "As for me, I said in my prosperity, 'I shall never be moved.'" David could rest secure because he was prosperous or, as other translations put it, resting at peace and untroubled. He did all the right things to secure himself against trouble.

At least, he thought he had. In the middle of verse 7, David suddenly shifts: "By your favor, O God, you had established me as a strong mountain; you hid your face, I was dismayed."

David had a downturn, to say the least. His prosperity amounted to nothing when suffering came, dismaying David and his life. The security David felt from his prosperity turned out to amount to nothing. It couldn't save him from trouble when it came. Prosperity couldn't provide for him when life turned nasty. David has apparently done nothing to deserve this, either. The cause of David's trouble is God hiding his face, which is another way of saying that evil is having its way with David for the moment. Something has happened to dismay, or other translations say, to terrify, David.

He's terrified. God seems absent and far away. He's in a moment of disorientation, where the darkness settles in and God seems far away. Times of disorientation are times where there are no answers and we can't seem to find our way back to the old ways, the past, the times of orientation, where things were good. During those times of orientation, the world seems like it's orderly. Disorientation reveals the chaos of the world that's always there, lurking beneath the surface. In our prosperity, we forget that it is there, believing that we shall never be moved.

In those times of disorientation, we wonder to ourselves if we can ever experience life as good, hopeful, and orderly again. Most of all, our sense of security evaporates. During times of orientation, we thought we were secure against the threats of the world. Disorientation reveals just how vulnerable we are. And we don't like being vulnerable.

So we ask: How do we create security for ourselves?

After all, insurance only goes so far. If one of the four of us in my family dies, life insurance will pay for costs and provide financial security, but it can't resurrect my loved one. There's still tremendous loss. If fire destroys my home, insurance will buy me a new TV but can't replace Dana's grandparents' dining room set that we cherish as a family heirloom. If a life-upending diagnosis hits me, as I have known these last several months, disability insurance can replace my income but can't replace the sense of purpose and satisfaction I derive from my profession.

Insurance can only go so far. We do our best to be prepared, but our preparation can only go so far. There's always the threat of the event that will undo all of our best planning. There's always the fear of that thing that we can't control happening. Our best security preparations, no matter how prosperous we are as individuals or as a country, can only go so far.

Perhaps that describes your reality as you read: an event that has undone good planning, something we cannot control and feared happening. Such change, such suffering, rocks our security. Whether we planned well and felt secure, or even if we lived a life held together with duct tape, we still all experience the loss of security when suffering comes, especially the disorienting, turn-your-life-upside-down kind of suffering.

And so, we will from time to time experience evil in the world. Perhaps it's a job loss like I've known, or a grave illness that threatens. Maybe it's a lost relationship with a spouse or parent. Perhaps it's actions someone or a group took against you or someone you hold dear. Evil happens to us, a reality David knew well. It made him cry out in verse 10, "Hear, O Lord, and be gracious to me! O Lord, be my helper!"

The Psalms as a book know this reality well. Suddenly the darkness comes and overwhelms because evil has wrought its destruction. Suddenly our sense of security evaporates. Suddenly evil seems to be winning. How can we create security for ourselves?

I am a big fan of the Taizé Community in France; it's an ecumenical monastery that inspires me in many ways. Perhaps the most inspirational story for me is what they did when they lost security—when their founder was brutally murdered.[3]

On an unremarkable day a few decades ago, the founder of Taizé, Brother Roger, was leading worship just as he always did three times a day. A woman walked into the chapel during worship, down the center aisle, and stabbed him brutally in front of the congregation. She then ran out and was quickly apprehended by the police.

We can imagine the response of the crowd, the horror, the earth-shattering sudden disruption of reality. For the monks of the monastery, those who knew Brother Roger best and had helped cultivate this space of peace and Christian unity, this one act turned their lives upside down. Change came suddenly, viciously, cruelly upon the Taizé community.

Yet their response forms an inspirational tale. Brother Roger founded the monastery on the principle of reconciliation. They desire to see all Christians from around the world reconciled together, in unity. Taizé believes in fostering love and harmony through forgiveness and the restoration of relationship. As such, they highly value being an open community that anyone can attend.

When violence happened, those values came under direct threat. Could they remain open when their founder was murdered?

Their answer was a resounding yes. In response to the murder, the monastery changed none of its security measures, in that they continued to have no security measures. They then went and offered the murderer their forgiveness as she sat in her jail cell. The monks visited the parents of the murderer saying to them that they desired to grieve together, for they knew her parents didn't desire their child to grow up and commit such a heinous act.

They acted out of their values for reconciliation and openness. They could do so because they have this fundamental Christian conviction: Suffering will happen until Christ comes in final victory. We can't control that. We can't stop that. But we can be faithful when suffering occurs in our lives, when the chaos ensues, because we know that no matter what happens to us, God will redeem it.

They embraced that change will come, disorientation will happen, and sometimes our worlds will be turned upside down. They understood that, ultimately, the answer to the question of how we create security for ourselves is that we cannot.

This is yet another reality we must accept. Like expecting hardship and change, we must expect to lose security. As we invite the suffering to pull up a chair to the table of our hearts, we accept that we cannot create the security we long for, that we desire.

David is highly aware of this. After reporting how he cried out during his disaster, he remarks to us, "You, God, have turned my mourning into dancing; you have taken off my sackcloth and clothed me with joy, so that my soul may praise you and not be silent. O Lord my God, I will give thanks to you forever." That's where he ends: It was God who restored, God who provided, God who moved in power. It was God who restored security.

And, indeed, it is only God ultimately who can offer us that sense of security. Insurance, preparedness plans, and security measures all have their place. I will continue to pay my insurance premiums and encourage preparedness because it is common sense.

But we lack sufficient control to prevent a loss of security. Accepting our inability to create security means accepting that we have limited control in this life. In fact, the more I live life on this earth, the less I think I can control. There remains that cosmic battle between good and evil, one in which we all get caught up at times. Why God allows evil to happen to us, no one can fully answer. But the fact remains that suffering will occur and security will give way to insecurity, but the truth of our lives is that, because God is with us, insecurity will eventually lead to a new security.

God promises us that new security. It's God's good pleasure to provide for us, to suddenly bring us to a new and surprising place of security. David experienced this. At the end of the Psalm, he declares, "You have turned my mourning into dancing; you have taken off my sackcloth and clothed me with joy, so that my soul may praise you and not be silent. O Lord my God, I will give thanks to you forever."

After rhetorically asking God, "What profit is there in my death … ? Will the dust praise you? Will it tell of your faithfulness? Hear, O Lord … be my helper," David declares that God has done a surprising new thing, restoring David, bringing him through the time of suffering into a new security.

So it is for us. God brings us to new security on the other side of the land of suffering. We will find ourselves surprised by this turn to security, this restoration.

Look back in the memory of your relationship with God and see how God has brought you through tough times to a place of restoration, healing, and security. In those moments, life looks different; your relationship with God is different, better, because you can see how God has moved in tremendous ways. We all have these stories. I have such stories. And in chapter 15, we will examine just how to use the past to fuel our present trek through the land of suffering. Suffice to say for now, God will restore again because God has restored in the past. God will because God has.

Which means, in the darkest nights of our lives, we can believe that light will shine again, just as it has done in past darknesses. And, after all, that's what faith is: "Believing in advance what will only make sense in reverse."[4] The task for today, as you read and as I write, caught as we are in our own moments of disorientating suffering, is to accept that we cannot create the security we want. We lack sufficient control. Only God can restore us to security, and God controls the timing. Yet we know that God is faithful, God will provide. No matter the darkness we know, the light shines.

In these moments of insecurity, I often cling to the words written by the priest Phillips Brooks so many years ago: "Yet in thy dark streets shineth the everlasting light; the hopes and fears of all the years are met in thee tonight."[5]

The hopes and fears of even this moment, this day, this present suffering, are met in God today. And so we can say with David, "Even though I walk through the darkest valley, I fear no evil [or suffering!], for you [God] are with me" (Psalm 23:4).

Field Notes

It's so tempting to try to create security! Are there ways you are trying to create security for yourself or loved ones today? Record those here, then give them to God in prayer, surrendering your attempt at control and embracing that only God can create the security we crave.

CHAPTER 6

Expect Relational Disruption

"They compelled a passer-by, who was coming in from the country, to carry his cross; it was Simon of Cyrene, the father of Alexander and Rufus. Then they brought Jesus to the place called Golgotha (which means Place of a Skull). And they offered him wine mixed with myrrh, but he did not take it. And they crucified him and divided his clothes among them, casting lots to decide what each should take."—Mark 15:21-24

HAVE YOU EVER SAVED UP your money to make a big trip? I imagine we all have at some point. My brother and I did that for several years, leading up to our trip to Scotland in 2021. We had a blast, saw so many really amazing things, touched history in powerful ways, and thoroughly enjoyed ourselves.

Traveling can do that. We see beyond ourselves to witness something different, hopefully something amazing. We get taken to a perspective beyond our usual surroundings to see the world with fresh eyes. And when we go travel somewhere, it's for an important reason—to explore, to get away, to visit family and friends, to be enchanted.

I remember traveling to Venezuela for a missions class in seminary, with pit stops in Aruba and Curaçao. Both were amazing, beautiful islands, and I found myself longing to return some day and stay for a long time. I was enchanted. At the Curaçao airport, customs was downstairs from the terminals. Walking around and exploring, I noticed that customs was completely unmanned, the lights even dark. I could have walked right through, out the doors just beyond the passport check stations, and entered Curaçao unencumbered. For a split second, I even thought about it! Then reason took back over, and I walked back upstairs.

Sometimes, traveling has that kind of enchanting effect, where we've gone somewhere that we fall in love with and a part of us wants to stay forever. Sometimes, traveling is enchanting because we're finally at a place we've dreamed of forever, a place we've longed to go visit, and finally the day has arrived.

Traveling is enchanting. So it was for Simon the Cyrene. Mark identifies Simon as a Cyrene, which identifies him from a region in North Africa, in modern-day Libya. If you know your geography, you know that Libya is pretty far down the Mediterranean coast from Jerusalem, where he is in our scripture this morning. As much as travel in Ancient Rome was easier than in the rest of the world at that time, this is still a far, risky distance to travel. In fact, it's the equivalent of driving from Macon, Georgia, where I live, to Phoenix, Arizona.

Except, of course, Simon didn't drive. He probably walked part, rode a mule for part, and took a ship for part. But all of that was fraught with danger. There were bandits on the roads that were ready to rob you and beat you up. Think of the story of the Good Samaritan. The Samaritan rescues a man who's been left on the side of the road, beaten up by robbers. Jesus uses that illustration because it was so common to find someone like this Samaritan—robbed, beaten up, left on the side of the road. Then, as if that wasn't bad enough, there were storms on the Mediterranean that could come out of nowhere and wreck a ship. If you remember Acts, that's exactly what happened to Paul, and it was a common occurrence for ancient travelers.

So traveling was hard, dangerous, exhausting work. And by foot, mule, and boat, Simon has traveled from Phoenix to Macon, from Cyrene to Jerusalem.

Consider as well that this trip is probably a once-in-a-lifetime event for Simon, one that he has saved up for years in order to make.

There was a large Jewish community in ancient Cyrene. For many Jews across the Roman Empire, there was no place more special than the second temple, the one rebuilt on the foundation of Solomon's Temple, in the center of Jerusalem. And there was no time of year more special than Passover.

So Simon, a Jew and member of this community in Cyrene, having probably saved for a lifetime, embarks on this long journey to Jerusalem to visit the temple at Passover. It's a religious pilgrimage, the trip of a lifetime! We can imagine he's excited, he's thrilled, he's ecstatic, he's enchanted, as only travel can do. Think of the last time you left for a big trip, maybe the trip of a lifetime: How excited you were, how grateful you were to go, how thrilled you were at the thought of finally getting to go to the place of your dreams.

Add to these excited feelings a religious fervor. Simon is going to worship God and remember God's salvation through the exodus at the temple in the holy city of Jerusalem at Passover. No previous Passover in Simon's life could be so great as this one. Not only is he probably excited, but he feels the joy and peace that comes from anticipating a wonderful, holy moment with God. This is the trip of a lifetime! Perhaps he anticipates that it will be the greatest moment of his life as he makes the long journey to Jerusalem.

Simon, as he arrives at Jerusalem, is looking forward to the hopes and dreams of all the years coming true—to experiencing this trip of a lifetime.

When he finally gets to Jerusalem, as he is coming into town, a Roman soldier taps Simon on the shoulder with a spear. That's the universal signal in Roman times compelling an individual for a task on behalf of the Roman military. And when you're tapped on the shoulder with a spear, when Rome compels you, you cannot say no. Simon must do whatever the Roman soldier tells him to do.

There's Jesus, walking down the Via Dolorosa, carrying the crossbeam of the cross where he will hang. He's been beaten up by soldiers, taunted, tortured, and now he's having to carry a large, heavy, piece of wood. We don't know if Jesus stumbles, if he's just too exhausted to go on, or what the reason is. But when the soldier taps Simon on the shoulder with his spear, it's to tell Simon he must carry the crossbeam for Jesus.

Simon's trip of a lifetime, the one he's saved for, the one he's anticipated for so long, the one he risked the perils of travel to make, enchanting as he expected it to be, has turned into a nightmare.

Consider that Simon knows nothing of what's happened before this moment. He knows nothing of the sham trial before Caiaphas and Pilate, he knows nothing of the crowds chanting to give them Barabbas and crucify Jesus. He probably has never even heard of Jesus and certainly wouldn't recognize him. Jesus has been a minor celebrity just in Galilee and Jerusalem, thousands of miles from Cyrene.

So Simon knows nothing of any of this and nothing of Jesus, either. He's a complete and total outsider, thrust into drama he did not choose.

He's done nothing wrong, nothing to deserve this. All he did was travel to Jerusalem on a religious pilgrimage, the trip of a lifetime, and have the bad luck of showing up at the wrong time. Simon is simply and horrifyingly thrust into a drama he did not choose.

As we consider our journey through the land of suffering, perhaps we can relate.

We have known drama that we did not choose but got thrust into anyway. The workplace is famous for that. Maybe we get promoted and someone else, who thinks they deserved it, doesn't. Factions break out. Tensions rise. Lines are drawn. Or maybe it's the reverse: Someone else gets promoted and you think you deserved it. The result is the same. Either way, you didn't ask for that drama. It just happened, and you find relationships disrupted, thrust into drama you did not choose.

Or, at the workplace, a new boss comes in and changes everything. Seemingly overnight, your whole world at work changes. That happened to me in my past. I was thrust into drama I didn't choose, which turned out to be a painful experience, disrupting relationships as people kept distance from me and my newfound drama.

It happens in families, too. We didn't choose for our parents to get divorced but it happened, and we found ourselves caught in the middle. Or we didn't choose for our parents to get very sick and need lots of care and attention, creating drama around who's spending enough time with mom and dad or who's paying for all the care and things like that, driving a wedge between siblings. There are many ways we can get caught up in family drama we did not choose, leading to disruption in these fundamental, foundational relationships.

It also happens wherever people are gathered together in community. We've known drama we did not choose on boards of community organizations, at church, at commission meetings, at the club, at Rotary, at the gym, and all sorts of other places. Like a former professor of mine once said: Politics is just a fancy word for relationships. And relationships sometimes bring drama, including drama we did not choose but drama we're caught up in anyway.

Life can thrust us into drama we did not choose, like Simon the Cyrene. And when that happens, it disrupts relationships in our lives. Most recently, I have found that drama with the committee at the church I last served who voted to seek a new senior pastor, having grown impatient with my health challenges. People I thought I knew well, people I thought I could trust, people I thought supported me and my family, acted completely contrary to those notions. How could they do that? I do not know, but I do know it thrust my family into drama we did not choose, disrupting and even severing those relationships.

Sometimes, life thrusts us into drama we did not choose, disrupting relationships and expectations. That's what happened to Simon the Cyrene. That simple tap by a Roman soldier thrust him into the drama of the crucifixion, something he did not choose but was also unable to avoid. So Simon grabs the crossbeam, unable to do otherwise. He carries it all the rest of the way to Golgotha, going through this hardship, this suffering—forced into drama he did not choose.

This is the case in life. The actions of others will thrust us into drama we did not choose, like the tap of this Roman soldier on Simon's shoulder. People we don't know will make decisions that affect us negatively, sometimes severely, creating suffering in our lives. Other times, people we do know, people we know well, will take action or make decisions that betray our sense of relationship, our trust, thrusting us into drama we did not choose, harming or even severing the relationship.

What do we do when thrust into drama we did not choose?

What do we do when our families erupt in drama and we didn't choose it, but we're caught up in it anyway? What do we do when our workplaces erupt in drama and we didn't choose it, but we're caught up in it anyway? What do we do when our civic organizations or community boards or volunteer agencies or clubs and gyms erupt in drama and we didn't choose it, but we're caught up in it anyway? What do we do when our society, whether here locally or across the country, erupts in drama and we didn't choose it, but we're caught up in it anyway?

What do we do when the decisions and actions of others cause us to suffer?

What do we do when thrust into drama we did not choose?

To get at the answer to that question, let's fast-forward the story here in Mark about twenty or thirty years. At that point, churches have formed in people's houses. There's a need for people like Mark to write a gospel so these churches can read and learn about the teachings and story of Jesus. Paul is traveling around the Roman Empire, preaching and founding churches, writing letters to them that eventually become books like 1 Corinthians and Ephesians. Christianity isn't called Christianity yet, but instead The Way, and it's spreading like wildfire around the eastern side of the Roman Empire, down into Egypt and up into Greece.

The Way at this point is so small that the leaders of the movement are well known to churchgoers. These leaders come and visit to encourage and instruct, traveling around from church to church, just like Methodist clergy. They itinerate, and when they're not traveling, they're writing letters like Paul did.

So notice with me how Mark identifies Simon the Cyrene. Note first that we have his name and where he's from. That's remarkable in and of itself. Simon is an outsider, someone who has just arrived in Jerusalem for the Passover, and yet Mark knows his name. Simon didn't drop the crossbeam at Golgotha and walk away. If he had, history wouldn't remember his name, much less where he came from. Mark names Simon because Mark knows Simon and expects that his readers know Simon, too.

Not only that, but Mark identifies Simon as "the father of Alexander and Rufus." That means Mark expects his readers will not only know of Simon, but that they'll also be familiar with Simon's sons, Alexander and Rufus. These are not random people whose names somehow got preserved. There are many characters across scripture, and especially in the New Testament, whose names we do not know. But that's not the case here. Mark knows Simon, Alexander, and Rufus. Mark expects those names to be known by his readers. That's why he identifies them, because he wants his readers to know the backstory of three people they probably already know.

Which means this: Simon, Alexander, and Rufus are probably leaders of the early church.

In fact, other New Testament books witness to two of these three. Paul refers to a man named Rufus in Romans 16, calling him "eminent in the Lord," apparently a leader of the church in Rome. In Acts 13, Simeon of Niger is listed among those sent out on a church mission from Antioch. Simeon is just a different way of saying Simon, and Niger, at this point in history, refers to the region around Cyrene. So it's possible that the missionary in Acts 13 is the same Simon in Mark 15 and that Rufus in Romans 16 is the same as the one mentioned here, the son of Simon the Cyrene, aka Simeon of Niger.

I love the thought that these men show up later in our history, in the New Testament, as leaders of the church. There's no way to prove that definitively; we just don't know enough about them. But regardless of whether the Rufus and Simeon of Romans and Acts are the same as those listed here in Mark, these three names are known leaders to the early Christian community. They're obviously important people who were known by the early church; otherwise, Mark would not have named Simon, much less his sons. He only does so because he expects his readers will immediately identify with them, knowing them from the growing Christian movement they called The Way. And it's very possible that their conversion to Christianity began here, with Simon's trip of a lifetime turning into a nightmare, as he's compelled to carry the cross of Christ, experiencing drama he didn't choose.

It means that this Simon, mentioned by Mark, and his sons became Christians because Simon was thrust into drama he did not choose. And not only that, it means that Simon most likely became a leader of the early church and inspired his sons to do the same because Simon was thrust into a drama he did not choose.

If that Roman soldier had never tapped Simon on the shoulder, turning his trip of a lifetime into a nightmare, the church would have been robbed of three of its early leaders.

Simon was thrust into drama he did not choose. But God turned what was meant for evil into a powerful good.

So what do we do when we are thrust into drama that we did not choose?

We, like Simon, carry the cross of Christ, believing that God will redeem the drama we did not choose and will create something good out of the relational disruption we know.

Simon was converted by having to carry the cross of Christ. Apparently, he stayed at Golgotha, picked up the story of Jesus, learned about the man, and was converted. His sons, as a result, were converted, and probably became the church leaders referred to by both Mark and Paul. God did an amazing work of redemption in their lives.

So it will be with us. The promise here in the story of Simon the Cyrene is the promise of God's redemption. Sometimes, we get thrust into drama we didn't choose. It happens to all of us from time to time. And sometimes, the drama we get thrust into is overwhelming, dark, difficult, unbearable even—much like we can imagine carrying the crossbeam was for Simon.

But God will do a powerful work of redemption through us. Consider that the cross itself is the ultimate symbol of God's redemption, of God's power to turn evil into good. God took a symbol of execution, of the power of Rome, and made it into a universally recognized symbol of hope and of God's good power. The cross went from a sign of death to a sign of life and life abundant.

That's what God does. God takes what was meant for evil and turns it to good. God will provide in powerful ways. We must walk on through the land of suffering, carrying the cross that's been thrust upon us, until we reach the finish line. And we have to do that, like Simon, without knowing where the finish line is.

This is a tough message. None of us want to hear that we must do what we don't want to do.

I'm an eight on the Enneagram. That's the chief thing you don't do to an eight—eights will not be controlled. I feel that deeply; I react strongly when I feel like I'm being controlled. But even if you're not an eight like me, none of us want to be told that we must do what we don't want to do, much less that we must suffer against our will by being thrust into drama we didn't choose. None of us want the pain of disruption to relationships in our lives, nor the loss of relationship that sometimes accompanies such suffering.

But Jesus himself told us that we would. Jesus himself says that to take up our cross daily and follow him will be costly. And part of that cost, part of that suffering, is when we don't choose to take up a particular cross but—instead, like Simon—find it thrust upon us.

Recent days have come with the challenge of accepting the actions of this church committee. As much as I had no choice, like Simon's compulsory service, I still wrestled with it. Such is natural: We don't want to accept that this bad thing has happened. To accept it means to admit the drama is real, the disruption to relationships true. Our minds struggle to conform to this sudden, new, and jarring reality. Yet this is the first step. Just as we've seen in previous chapters, acceptance forms the beginning of moving forward.

Then, when we have accepted, we must continue walking forward, journeying through the land of suffering. Part of that process will be practicing forgiveness, a topic discussed in chapter 16. But before we can get there, we must take care of ourselves, processing how this drama we did not choose and its corresponding relational disruption have changed our realities. We must assess the harm done, consider the consequences, and focus in on self-care.

We can do so knowing God will redeem the actions of others that have caused harm by thrusting us into drama we did not choose. Simon and his sons are examples of that. God did a new and surprising work through this sudden disruption to Simon's life. For me, as I apply for jobs and wait to see what God will do next, I hold true to the promise that God is doing something new. To step forward is to live into the lines of the hymn, "This Is a Day of New Beginnings":

> Then let us, with the Spirit's daring,
> step from our past and leave behind
> our disappointment, guilt, and grieving,
> seeking new paths, and sure to find
> Christ is alive, and goes before us,
> to show and share what love can do.
> This is a day of new beginnings;
> our God makes all things new.[6]

While I cannot yet see how God is making all things new, I can step from my past and continue to move forward, bearing my cross, confident that God is at work, actively redeeming these circumstances.

The early Christian movement wouldn't have been the same without Simon, Alexander, and Rufus. God made something amazingly good out of drama Simon did not choose. So it will be for you and for me.

In the midst of the drama and relational disruption you know, especially drama you did not choose, cling to that belief. Take up your cross and follow Jesus. Redemption is coming. God will turn your suffering—the cross you bear, the one you did not ask for—into a powerful good for the world.

Field Notes

How have the decisions or actions of others led to your journey through the land of suffering? Declare that here, moving toward acceptance of this reality. How can you imagine God redeeming these circumstances? Can you already see God at work, moving in redemption power?

Chapter 7

Expect Fear

"Now the Philistines gathered their armies for battle; they were gathered at Socoh, which belongs to Judah, and encamped between Socoh and Azekah, in Ephes-dammim. Saul and the Israelites gathered and encamped in the valley of Elah and formed ranks against the Philistines. The Philistines stood on the mountain on the one side, and Israel stood on the mountain on the other side, with a valley between them. And there came out from the camp of the Philistines a champion named Goliath, of Gath, whose height was four cubits and a span. He had a helmet of bronze on his head, and he was armed with a coat of mail; the weight of the coat was five thousand shekels of bronze. He had greaves of bronze on his legs and a javelin of bronze slung between his shoulders. The shaft of his spear was like a weaver's beam, and his spear's head weighed six hundred shekels of iron, and his shield-bearer went before him. He stood and shouted to the ranks of Israel, 'Why have you come out to draw up for battle? Am I not a Philistine, and are you not servants of Saul? Choose a man for yourselves, and let him come down to me. If he is able to fight with me and kill me, then we will be your servants, but if I prevail against him and kill him, then you shall be our servants and serve us.' And the Philistine said, 'Today I defy the ranks of Israel! Give me a man, that we may fight together.' When Saul and all Israel heard these words of the Philistine, they were dismayed and greatly afraid."—1 Samuel 17:1-11

THE HARDSHIP, CHANGE, AND INSECURITY we know through suffering elicits fear. Relational drama can bring its own fear, as we find what we thought were solid relationships disrupted, bringing suffering.

On my own journey, I have often experienced fear. What will come next? Will I ever fully recover? Will this immunodeficiency define the rest of my life? Will I find a job? Will there be a church for me to serve? Will we have to move? How much more can I take? The fear overwhelms, threatening to consume me.

We should expect fear when journeying through the land of suffering, and yet fear is perhaps harder to handle than anything we have examined so far. Fear blinds, like a sandstorm or a blizzard, threatening to cause us to lose our way. We might hear that fear is not of God, and that is true, but how do we find our way when fear envelops?

To begin, let us consider the story of Robert Wadlow, the Giant of Illinois.

Born in 1918, he grew to be the tallest man who ever lived. At least, the tallest we can confirm. Because of a disease of his pituitary gland that was incurable at the time, he produced massive amounts of the human growth hormone. This caused his body to grow to the astounding height of eight feet eleven inches.

By some accounts, Goliath was even larger. He stood, according to scripture, at six cubits and a span. There's some disagreement about how tall that is exactly because there's disagreement about just how long a cubit was. But we can say Goliath was at least six feet, seven inches—quite tall, especially considering humans were generally shorter in his day than they are today. But by some accounts, Goliath was as tall as nine feet, nine inches, even taller than the Giant of Illinois.

His compatriots, the Philistine Army, stand behind this giant, ready to go to battle. Across the valley, the Israelite army sits encamped, too, ready for battle. Goliath comes out and not only challenges them, but taunts them in a way that evokes fear from King Saul and the Israelites: "When Saul and all Israel heard these words of the Philistine, they were dismayed and greatly afraid" (1 Samuel

17:11). And rightly so. Goliath is more than just a giant. They have three big reasons to be dismayed and greatly afraid of him, to be consumed by fear.

First, Goliath is huge. We've already noted his height—tall for our time and even more so for his time when people simply did not grow as tall as we do. But not only this, scripture notes that he's a champion—a Hebrew word that literally means "he stands between." He can stand between two men and not be taken down. He's a battle-hardened warrior; probably with big muscles and the intimidating stance and presence that any champion warrior would have. Goliath is huge.

Second, he's overwhelming. The scripture goes to great lengths to describe his armor. It's the best the Israelites have ever seen and probably represents some technology they didn't have. This would be intimidating enough. What armor will the Israelites use against him? What weapons? They're overwhelmed by the challenge. Not only that, but when he says, "Today, I defy the ranks of Israel," he's insulting them. He's saying, "Today I disgrace, I shame, I spit on the ranks of Israel." He's so confident in himself that he believes there is no defeating him. This is a psychological victory, for the very next verse indicates that King Saul and all of Israel are indeed intimidated by this disgrace, this shame. They cannot stand against him. Goliath is overwhelming.

Third, the stakes are high. In the ancient world of Saul and Goliath, a single fight between two warriors would sometimes determine the outcome of an entire battle. In Goliath's challenge, there's more than just egos involved. Should Goliath win against Israel's best warrior, all of Israel could be defeated and thus become servants of the Philistines. At a very minimum, Goliath's victory would give a huge psychological advantage to the Philistine army ahead of the ensuing battle between both nation's armies. The stakes are very high.

Goliath is more than just a giant. In confronting Goliath, the Israelite army is facing a huge, overwhelming, high-stakes challenge.

It's no wonder that "Saul and all Israel … were dismayed and greatly afraid."

It's only human to react in just that way in the face of such a challenge. It's only human to react with fear.

And isn't that the case whenever we face serious challenges, especially of the variety caused by suffering? Confronted with some huge, overwhelming, and high-stakes challenge, don't we also become dismayed and greatly afraid?

Certainly we do. We can relate to Saul and all of Israel as they face down this giant whose challenge is huge, overwhelming, and high stakes, for we have known Goliaths of our own: a terrible diagnosis, perhaps of cancer or some other disease; a close relationship with a friend or family member that is failing and seems inevitably headed for separation; a family conflict that threatens to turn legal, or that results in hurt and broken relationships; a financial loss that threatens the foundation of our families or businesses or institutions we love and support; or perhaps an internal wrestling we keep that we dare not tell others, lest they think poorly of us, but still the secret destroys us internally.

And sometimes, these huge, overwhelming, high-stakes challenges grow over time, leaving us wondering how much more we can take, fearful of the next shoe dropping. Living in such fear sometimes indicates the presence of trauma, where our outlook is skewed toward expecting and anticipating the next hardship.

These last several months have been like that for me and my family.

A few months before I got sick, I had a bout of bad anxiety, brought on by witnessing a significant act of violence. As that was receding, Dana had surgery with its challenges. Then we had a friend who was living with cancer suddenly get very sick, decline rapidly, and pass away in September. At the same time, I labored to run a stewardship campaign, add additional household duties while Dana recovered, and deal with my own emotional and psychological weariness. For about three months, I had quite a season of stress. As the challenges built, they increasingly felt like Goliath: huge, overwhelming, and high stakes.

Little did I know those three months were just the beginning. Not long after our friend passed away, I got COVID, which launched my current journey. The suffering I knew gave way to deeper suffering, furthering my sense that I faced huge, overwhelming, high-stakes challenges. As I was just starting to recover, Jackson fell ill. While he was sick, I started to grow worse. Then came the diagnosis and hope. Then Jackson grew worse and the church I served grew difficult. Then, just as Jackson was finally recovering and I could see light at the end of the tunnel with the start of treatments, the church voted me out. Sometimes, these huge, overwhelming, high-stakes challenges come on all at once, and sometimes they develop over time. All of it elicits fear, and that fear sometimes leads to trauma.

In all of this, what are we to do in the face of those challenges?

Put another way, when Goliaths appear in our lives, how should we respond?

First, we should respond like Saul and the Israelites, with dismay and fear. That may sound surprising but, if we don't, we're not human. Those emotions are not wrong and, indeed, they're useful from a psychological perspective. They help us process, and they activate parts of our brain that keep us safe.

Sometimes when we're facing these kinds of huge, overwhelming, high stakes challenges, we hear that Christians are somehow not supposed to react with fear and dismay, that somehow we're just supposed to shrug our shoulders or stand resolute, unmoved by our cancer diagnosis, failing family relationships, threat of financial ruin, or some problem deep in our soul. Or when the things of life build up and life feels huge, overwhelming, and high stakes, we're somehow supposed to have a stiff upper lip as Christians and not experience these very human emotions of dismay and fear. Too often, as Christians we hear messages that we're not supposed to experience trauma. Nothing could be further from the truth.

God designed us to have these emotions as part of our fight or flight response. We should feel these things. We should respond in that way when these huge, overwhelming, high-stakes challenges appear in our lives. It's part of how God designed us, and it helps keep us safe.

So the question is not whether we should experience fear. We should and we do and we will. The question instead is whether or not the fear defines us. When we face huge, overwhelming, high-stakes challenges, do we allow fear to have the last word?

That's the issue for Saul and all Israel. Fear defined Saul. In response to the challenge of Goliath, he went into his tent and sulked. We can imagine him wringing his hands in dismay, desperate for a solution but believing none exists. All the Israelites ran in fear back to their tents after catching sight of Goliath, saying to one another, "Have you seen [him]?" (1 Samuel 17:24-25) with much fear and trembling.

That's how they stay: in a state of fear. And that's what fear does when it defines us: it immobilizes and causes us to sulk in self-pity. Fear can be, on its own, huge, overwhelming, and high stakes. Sometimes the fear becomes worse than the challenge itself, as it blinds us to solutions and blinds us to how God is moving in power around us.

We will first react with fear whenever a huge, overwhelming, high-stakes challenge confronts us. That's just human and how God designed us. But then, we have a choice about whether or not the fear will define us.

As the Goliath story progresses, we discover that David, a boy of little regard and reputation, is the solution. God has provided a way out for the Israelites. David slays the giant. Then, flush with the psychological victory, the Israelite army rushes forward and carries the day in battle.

Sometimes, we get to see God move in power like that. Our faith proclaims that God will deliver us just as God delivered the Israelites. It's easy to look back and say how we saw God move in power after God has delivered us from our huge, overwhelming, high-stakes challenges. Certainly, that's what God does. That hindsight fuels our faith—we know that if God has before, God can do it again.

But life is at its toughest when fear is present, when we face those huge, overwhelming, high-stakes challenges and don't know what to do next. While we're in fear, we have no idea what that deliverance will look like. These are the moments when fear seems to blind us like a sandstorm or blizzard, obscuring the way forward as we journey through suffering. So what do we do while we're waiting for that deliverance? Because it sure can feel like it takes a long time before God delivers, especially when fear is present.

This is especially true when the challenges we face are like how we've described Goliath: huge, overwhelming, and high stakes. Those terrible health diagnoses; the failing familial relationships, especially those failing marriage relationships; the awful financial downturns that can affect those we love or even institutions we love; or the secrets we keep that eat us up from the inside; living with trauma; all of those and more can evoke tons of fear and leave us feeling helpless and hapless, defined by our fear.

When our Goliaths stand before us and seem immoveable, what do we do while we are waiting for God to deliver us from our Goliaths, from our huge, overwhelming, high-stakes challenges?

In his speech, Goliath calls the Israelites "servants of Saul." That should strike us as odd. The Israelites were never to be servants of a king. God rescued them from being servants to a king named pharaoh so they could be servants of God!

But they are acting like servants of Saul. In David's speech to Saul later in 1 Samuel 17, David repeatedly calls on God's name—the first time God is mentioned in this story at all. The lack of mention of God shows how Saul and David are focused differently. Saul is focused on his fear. David is focused on God.

And that difference in focus makes all the difference. In the midst of our fear, we must choose to focus on God instead of our fear. It will be very difficult, but focusing on God instead of our fear is how we keep fear from defining us while we await deliverance. Calling on God's name in the midst of the fear grants us sight through the sandstorm.

We will all face huge, overwhelming, high-stakes challenges from time to time. Those health diagnoses, failing familial relationships, family disputes, internal threats, or money troubles will hit all of us or those we love. They happen. Trauma happens. And our initial response will be fear, as it should be. But then, we must choose to focus on God instead of succumbing to the temptation to focus on our fears.

The ways we focus on God form the chapters of Part 2, where we see specific strategies for how to focus our minds, hearts, and energy toward our faith. In doing so, we find our way through the land of suffering. Suffice to say here that we focus through prayer and diligence in our relationship with God. Just as we saw in Chapter 2, all this book discusses finds its grounding in that divine-human relationship. Call on God's name and keep reading, discovering how to face down Goliaths in the land of suffering.

As we focus on what to expect in the land of suffering, we also note that we have a certain level of responsibility. While we must accept our limits, we yet have a role to play. When we wrestle and fight, refusing to accept the reality of suffering, we futilely expend energy that could help us, which only leaves us weak and blinded by fear. When we accept our suffering reality, inviting it to pull up a chair to the table of our hearts, we free that energy to go toward our relationship with God. And we must choose, we must be disciplined and attentive, in that relationship.

Such a focus does not cause God to act nor guarantee results we want. We do not have a transactional relationship with God. To focus on God, to be disciplined, is to draw our hearts nearer to their true home, where we find the sustenance we need for this journey through suffering.

Fear will come. We will all experience it. And fear is terrible. It's hard. On its own it is huge, overwhelming, and high stakes. Fear can be its own Goliath. But no matter the giants you face, the fear doesn't have to define.

In the face of fear, pray and get right with God. God, rather than fear, can define your journey through the land of suffering.

Field Notes

What fear do you know as you journey through the land of suffering? How can you take those fears in prayers to God?

Chapter 8

Expect a Valley Experience

"Six days later, Jesus took with him Peter and James and John and led them up a high mountain apart, by themselves. And he was transfigured before them, and his clothes became dazzling bright, such as no one on earth could brighten them. And there appeared to them Elijah with Moses, who were talking with Jesus. Then Peter said to Jesus, 'Rabbi, it is good for us to be here; let us set up three tents: one for you, one for Moses, and one for Elijah.' He did not know what to say, for they were terrified. Then a cloud overshadowed them, and from the cloud there came a voice, 'This is my Son, the Beloved; listen to him!' Suddenly when they looked around, they saw no one with them any more, but only Jesus. As they were coming down the mountain, he ordered them to tell no one about what they had seen, until after the Son of Man had risen from the dead."—Mark 9:2-9

We speak often as people of faith about mountaintop experiences. As I write, I can see the mountains of North Carolina nearby. They remind me of Psalm 121, "I lift my eyes to the hills—from where will my help come? My help comes from the Lord, who made heaven and earth" (Psalm 121:1-2). It's easy to feel God's presence and sense that God will help there on the mountaintop.

But what about when we come down the mountain into the valley? Life comes with valley experiences, too, but we speak of those less frequently. There, in the valley, we know the realities examined so far: hardship, change, insecurity, and fear. Perhaps we speak of valleys less often because they are hard and, unlike the mountaintop, God often seems far away or even absent. Valleys are not the topic of polite conversation; yet every mountaintop leads to a valley.

How do we find our way through the valley and back to the mountaintop?

Consider that there are two ways to the Berry College reservoir, a beautiful man-made lake on the 26,000 acres of mountainous property the college owns. Those two ways relate directly to the infamous choice of two paths: the easy way and the hard way.

The easy way is the wide, long path that goes from a former grist works called the Old Mill to the reservoir. It winds its way around a mountain summit, taking a longer but easier way to the reservoir. Just start walking past the gate and you'll get there after about a mile and a half, no problem.

The hard way, as Jackson and I learned one weekend, is straight up and over the mountain. Not long after the road begins, a trail starts off to the right of the main road that leads you straight up over a mountain summit and then back down. It's the shorter way, but the hard way.

We chose the hard way.

The hard way required us to hike up inclines that sometimes made it feel as though my toes were touching my shins; it was that steep. Jackson and I had to take frequent breaks.

But upon reaching the top of the mountain, it was all worth it. The views were breathtaking, with the glory and majesty of God's creation overwhelming in its full display. And the sense of accomplishment, of having done what had felt impossible at moments, was worth every difficult step.

Then back down the mountain we came, full of joy, seeing the reservoir come alive through the trees until we finally reached our goal, meeting up with Dana and Carter who had taken the wider, easier path.

In seeing the glory and majesty of God on full display in nature, Jackson and I had a mountaintop experience at that summit. I'm sure you can think of such mountaintop experiences in your own faith—times where you've experienced the glory and joy of the Lord on full display.

At the famous story of the transfiguration, that's exactly what the disciples Peter, James, and John are experiencing. They are having a certifiable mountaintop experience. Up on the mountain, these three disciples have met the two greatest figures of their faith: Moses and Elijah. Sight of these two overwhelms them with religious devotion. Imagine being up on a mountain where, suddenly, you know you're in the presence of Peter, James, and John. Imagine how you would react, how you would feel. That's how the disciples are feeling. They are completely consumed by the glory and honor of being in their presence.

Add to this that Jesus is transformed, or transfigured as we say, into his divine self. They see Jesus as he was and is—God. Then the voice of the Father speaks. On this one mountaintop, in this one moment, they experience the presence of the greats of Judaism, the sight of Jesus as God, and the voice of the Father.

It's unbelievable. It's one of the most incredible moments in scripture. Peter, James, and John are having what we can rightly call a mountaintop experience.

Have you ever had a mountaintop experience in your faith? Maybe not one so grand and overwhelming as this one from Mark, but a time when God's presence was so real and full? A time when you felt like you could reach out and touch God, when all the problems in your life, all the stresses, all the suffering, seemed to melt away? Moments in life when you knew, beyond a shadow of a doubt, that God is good, that God loves you, that God is with you?

I'm sure we all have. These are powerful moments, so powerful we're tempted to be like Peter, building our own shelters there on top of the mountain of faith, wanting to never leave that moment. And rightfully so, for there on the mountaintop we have experienced a bit of heaven on earth; we have experienced a bit of that unity with God for which we were designed. Who would ever want to leave?

The problem is these mountaintop experiences end.

Life comes with valley experiences, too. Times when, rather than experiencing God's presence as real and full, God feels absent. Times when, rather than reaching out and touching God, we wonder if God has bothered to show up at all. Moments when the Deist vision of a God who set the world in motion and then walked away feels right. Moments when we doubt, fully, that God is good, that God loves us, that God is with us.

These we call valley experiences, and we avoid them like the plague. And yet they keep occurring, often coming in the form of various suffering. We can rightly say that walking through the land of suffering is a valley experience.

I am walking a valley today and will be still tomorrow, writing as a way of finding my own way through the valley. Even today, I found myself feeling like I just wanted to get back to a time when things felt good and right and true. The question was, "How do I get back on top of the mountain?"

When we experience our own moments of life like this, how do any of us get back on top of the mountain? Back where we are fully convinced of God's faithfulness, of God's goodness, of God's presence? Back where everything seems to make sense? Back where life is easy and full of hope? In the midst of our valley experiences, we wonder: How do we get back there?

I can hear the disciples asking that same question. Our scripture reveals the valleys, as well as the mountaintops, of the life of faith.

Before this mountaintop experience, the disciples have been in the valley. Early in Jesus's ministry, he was very popular. Everyone wanted to be near this man who was full of wisdom and who could do miracles and wondrous signs. Jesus was the most popular man in Galilee—until he upset the Pharisees with his wisdom, until he upset the scribes with his reinterpretation of the law, until he upset the priests with his miracles.

Jesus, by this moment, has lost his popularity. He's now a rabble-rouser, a troublemaker, the leader of a faction of religious radicals.

No longer popular, no longer welcomed, and threatened by the religious establishment, he and the disciples have descended into the valley. And then, as if the valley weren't already dark enough, Jesus tells the disciples about his upcoming suffering and death, much to their dismay. The news of Jesus's suffering and death casts a shadow, the valley of the shadow of death, hanging over Peter and the disciples like a darkness that will not fade.

Then they leave the valley and go up the mountain. They see Moses and Elijah. They hear the voice of God who confirms Jesus's identity as God's very Son, Immanuel, God with them. They have the mountaintop experience!

But then they come back down the mountain, not to wonderful experiences but to Jesus rebuking the gathered crowd, calling them a "perverse generation." Jesus then forecasts his own death, again, bringing back the valley of the shadow of death—a valley that will not let up until the resurrection.

So the transfiguration is a brief mountaintop experience that comes in between two long valley experiences. I imagine the disciples Peter, James, and John found themselves wondering, "When can we go back up the mountain?"

The rises and falls of mountaintop and valley experiences, as with Peter, James, and John, are characteristic of the life of faith. We all experience it. Sometimes, when we're closer to the mountaintop, it's easy to accept that life is just that way. We hope we won't go back to the valley, but we're willing to accept that valleys happen because at the present moment life is good.

But other times, when we're closer to the valley, when the shadows of the valley overtake us, it's impossible to accept that this is just life. So impossible, in fact, that our faith begins to show signs of doubt. We begin to question God; we even become angry at God. We ask questions like: Why would a good God allow for suffering? Why would a faithful God allow us to live in the valley?

We are like David in Psalm 23, walking through the "valley of the shadow of death" (Psalm 23:4 KJV), wondering where God is and why we must suffer. The valleys are cold, dark, desolate, and lonely. They are full of fears, anxieties, despair, and disorientation. How are we to make sense of these moments? God, why? Come rescue us! Come to our aid!

But in the valleys, all too often, our cries seem to fall on deaf ears. How do we go up the mountain again?

In *The Silver Chair*, a book in the Chronicles of Narnia series by C. S. Lewis, Aslan speaks to the main character up on top of a mountain. You may recall that Aslan is Lewis's allegory for Jesus. So there, up on the mountain, Aslan shares these words about the life of faith, words we can imagine Jesus saying to us as we ask about our mountaintop and valley experiences of faith:

> Here on the mountain I have spoken to you clearly. I will not often do so down in Narnia. Here on the mountain, the air is clear and your mind is clear; as you drop down into Narnia, the air will thicken. Take great care that it does not confuse your mind. And the signs which you have learned here will not look at all as you expect them to look, when you meet them there. That is why it is so important to know them by heart and pay no attention to appearance. Remember the signs and believe the signs. Nothing else matters.[7]

Lewis speaks to the mountaintop reality: They are fleeting, they are wonderful, and once we leave them, the clarity and assurance we feel becomes complicated. Yet he also points to another reality: Those mountaintop experiences give us signs upon which we can rest our faith. They are part of our foundation of faith, ways we can "remember ... and believe" in God's faithfulness and goodness.

Today, whether on the mountaintop or in the valley, we have a sign to remember and believe, to give us hope no matter where we are in the journey of faith. That sign is the transfiguration.

Up on the mountaintop, the disciples saw Jesus for who he really was and is: the Son of God. He was transformed from his human self into his divine self. The disciples realized that Jesus is not some great prophet, not some reincarnation of Elijah; no, Jesus is far greater: Jesus is God, God made human, Emmanuel, a human who knows the mountaintops and valleys of life.

And that means the sign of the transfiguration isn't limited to the mountaintop experiences of life. The transfiguration tells us that God is with us in the valleys, too, because God has suffered alongside of us. God has walked, literally, through the valleys of life we have experienced. God has known the valleys of shadows so dark that the mountains are obscured. God has known the depths of human longing, of human anxiety. God has known what it is to be persecuted, beaten, unappreciated, maligned, and rejected. God has even doubted himself, experiencing what feels like the loss of God's presence, as Jesus cried out on the cross, "My God, My God, why have you forsaken me?" God has suffered.

Jesus has been where we are, no matter how dark the shadow cast over us in the valley, because Jesus walked willingly through those valleys. Jesus experienced the suffering we know all too well—the pain, anxiety, fear, loss, longing, rejection, and doubt of the valley moments of life.

The transfiguration is a sign to remind us that Jesus, God himself, came to be with us not only on the mountaintops, but especially in the valleys. God knows our suffering, God understands our suffering, because God has suffered as we have. God has been to the valley, too.

That means when you walk into the valley, God is with you, inside your very being through the presence of the Holy Spirit. And so we know, not only what David says about "walking through the valley of the shadow of death," but we also know the very next thing David says: "I will fear no evil: for thou art with me" (Psalm 23:4 KJV). In the valley moments, all we need do is turn inward to find God there, in the midst of the darkness and disorientation, in our suffering, saying, "I'm here, fear no evil, fear no darkness, fear no disorientation, fear no anxiety or pain or loss or longing or rejection or doubt. Fear not, for I am with you."

So let us take heart, for Christ is with us. He is with us in our hearts, he is with us in our loved ones, and he is with us through our churches. When we feel alone, when we feel God is far away, the transfiguration that revealed Jesus to be God is a sign of this promise: You are not alone, even in the valley.

How do we get back up the mountain?

Just like we cannot create security for ourselves, we also cannot take ourselves back up the mountain. These are gifts from God, like the apostles seeing Jesus transfigured. But while we wait, while we walk through the valley, we can take comfort knowing God Emmanuel. As we say at Advent, God with us.

However, we can "remember the signs and believe the signs," mindful of how God has provided for us before, of how God is faithful to us and good. Chapter 15 in particular points us in just that way, helping us see signs, remember the signs, and find there what we need to rest our belief that God is yet still faithful in the valley and God will provide for us as we journey through the land of suffering.

The transfiguration is a sign to us: a sign of hope because we know that God has suffered for us and continues to suffer with us. God does not destine us for evil, nor does God cause evil in our lives, but the valleys will come. Suffering will come.

My guess is, as you read this, you know suffering; you may be walking in a valley right now. We can take courage, take hope, for we know that God suffers with us because the God of our mountaintop experiences is the God of our valleys, too.

Field Notes

Define the valley you know today. What are its characteristics? Then, what signs do you know, or where do you see signs, that can fuel your faith?

CHAPTER 9

Expect Divine Empathy

"In the sixth month the angel Gabriel was sent by God to a town in Galilee called Nazareth, to a virgin engaged to a man whose name was Joseph, of the house of David. The virgin's name was Mary. And he came to her and said, 'Greetings, favored one! The Lord is with you.' But she was much perplexed by his words and pondered what sort of greeting this might be. The angel said to her, 'Do not be afraid, Mary, for you have found favor with God. And now, you will conceive in your womb and bear a son, and you will name him Jesus. He will be great and will be called the Son of the Most High, and the Lord God will give to him the throne of his ancestor David. He will reign over the house of Jacob forever, and of his kingdom there will be no end.' Mary said to the angel,'"How can this be, since I am a virgin?' The angel said to her, 'The Holy Spirit will come upon you, and the power of the Most High will overshadow you; therefore the child to be born will be holy; he will be called Son of God. And now, your relative Elizabeth in her old age has also conceived a son, and this is the sixth month for her who was said to be barren. For nothing will be impossible with God.' Then Mary said, 'Here am I, the servant of the Lord; let it be with me according to your word.' Then the angel departed from her."—Luke 1:26-38

THE GOD WE KNOW on the mountaintops of life is the same God who walks with us through the valley. The power of God's empathy comes through in the story of the birth of Jesus, coming in lowly human form, into Joseph and Mary's valley experience known as the census. As we wrestle with the hardship, change, insecurity, and fear we know in suffering, walking through the valley of the land of suffering, we discover that Christ is right there with us, a child of the poor who comes to us in our weakness. Perhaps it's there, in our weakness, that we come to best know who Jesus is in our lives, discovering the power of divine empathy. It's fair to say that we discover just exactly what child this is.

Throughout the Advent season, we sing carols like "What Child is This?" On Christmas Eve in particular, many of us sing one of the worst Christmas carols, in my opinion: "Silent Night." As my former staff would say, that's a hot take, but it remains my opinion, even as I have always closed Christmas Eve services with it. Consider the lyrics:

> Silent night, holy night,
> all is calm, all is bright,
> round yon virgin mother and child.
> Holy infant so tender and mild,
> sleep in heavenly peace,
> sleep in heavenly peace.[8]

It's a wonderful scene. This timeless hymn paints a beautiful picture. One can imagine the stars of the sky on a clear night shining down, a full moon providing its soft light onto a field where a cave pokes slightly out of a hillside. There in that cave is a young couple with their newborn child, smiling sweetly as he sleeps. What a wonderful, brilliant, beautiful scene.

In fact, it's really an astounding scene: God come into the world as an ordinary human baby to be Emmanuel, God with us. We're not wrong to ask, "What child is this?" wondering, with childish awe, how God could come in such a weak, frail, helpless form.

It's easy to imagine the shepherds asked the same question, wondering what child this is. If the old TV show Dirty Jobs had existed on Galilean TV back in Mary's day, shepherds would have certainly been featured. Like the folks who go into sewers, work landfills, and make cheese, shepherds were considered dirty. So they kept to themselves, on the outsides of cities, living their lives taking care of sheep.

These were, perhaps, some of the most ordinary people imaginable during Mary's day. And it's to these very ordinary people, these ostracized people, these outcasts, that God decides to make his big pronouncement. Like the king of England announcing the birth of a new prince or princess, God puts his royalty on full display in the night sky by sending a gaggle of angels out to the fields where, "Shepherds [were] keeping watch over their flock by night" (Luke 2:8). They put on an incredible show, an extraordinary show.

It's fair to say that the "Silent Night" version of this scene was probably right: "Silent night, holy night, shepherds quake at the sight; glories stream from heaven afar, heavenly hosts sing Alleluia."[9]

What child is this? A child who on Mary's lap is sleeping, whom angels greet with anthems sweet while shepherds watch are keeping? A child who looks for shelter among us, whom we see amidst the poor?

A few Advents ago, a friend shared with me a new carol titled "Child of the Poor." This particular version was a mash up, putting "Child of the Poor" with "What Child is This?" The first verse and chorus of "Child of the Poor" say this:

> Helpless and hungry, lowly afraid
> Wrapped in the chill of mid-winter,
> Comes now among us
> Born into poverty's embrace,
> new life for the world
> Who is this who lives with the lowly
> Sharing their sorrows, knowing their hunger?
> This is Christ, revealed to the world
> in the eyes of a child, a child of the poor[10]

Christ the King, who reigns in our hearts, lives with us as a friend and empathizes with all our human plights. Jesus, who was fully divine, came to earth to be fully human, to walk a mile in our shoes, which is the definition of empathy. We have a savior who can empathize with our human condition. This is Christ, revealed to the world in the eyes of a child, a child of the poor. This, this, is Christ the King!

How amazing and incredible that God would come to be one of us, experiencing life as we do, empathizing with our human condition. But what about those times when Jesus feels far away? Where we, ourselves, feel helpless, lonely, afraid, wrapped in the chill of midwinter? What about those times of suffering?

I have had several seasons like that, those that feel like midwinter. One in particular stands out. Many years ago, I left my counseling techniques class in a fog, completely lost. I aimlessly wandered around the campus of James Madison University. I couldn't go home; I wasn't sure why, but I just knew I couldn't go home yet. I was lonely and afraid, and Dana wasn't home yet, so I suppose the crowd of people around campus gave some small comfort.

I was in graduate school, pursuing a Master of Education in counseling, and had just shown a tape of me counseling a fellow student. I went into it thinking I'd done this magnificent job. I had solved the person's problems, provided sound advice, and told them what they should do next. Clearly, I was about to get all the praise and glory the professor could muster.

But of course, as any mental health professional knows from even my brief description, I'd done a terrible job. The professor raked me over the coals in front of my classmates. I left embarrassed, dejected, but also something deeper than that. Something had come loose inside me. There was a deeper breaking down that was happening, and I couldn't identify it.

I wandered around campus aimlessly, wrapped in the chill of midwinter. It was late January, there was snow on the ground, and my feet got wet from melting snow. I was chilled to the bone, but I hardly noticed; my suffering was so great it consumed me. I was helpless, afraid.

And where was God in the midst of my midwinter? Where was the help I needed? Where was the baby Christ who shares in our sorrows and knows our hunger? Where was this baby Jesus whom shepherds guard and angels sing? Where was God in the midst of my suffering?

What about those times where Jesus feels far away, where we, ourselves, feel helpless, lonely, afraid, wrapped in the chill of midwinter?

What child is this?

Consider how little we know about Jesus's life. We know something of his three years of ministry, leading up to his execution and resurrection. We know a little bit about his early years: his birth, the flight to Egypt, the visit of the magi, and the scene of him teaching in the temple as a boy. Otherwise, we know very little about his earthly life.

That's because Jesus, as a toddler, a little boy, a teenager, and finally a young man, was ordinary. He was the obscure son of a carpenter, learning to ply his father's trade. Based on the scene in the temple, we can imagine he had a reputation as being particularly talented at theology, and maybe his neighbors thought he would work in the temple one day. That would be no different from a child we know who's particularly talented at soccer or math or high in emotional intelligence; the kind of child for whom we have high expectations and see a clear career path. The point is that Jesus, prior to his ministry, was ordinary. And the whole of his earthly life, he was human, just as we are.

Knowing the ordinary circumstances of much of Jesus's life, we're right to ask the same question as that famous Christmas carol: What child is this? This child who "laid to rest, on Mary's lap is sleeping? Whom angels greet with anthems sweet while shepherds watch are keeping?"[11] His ordinary and obscure birth, announced in extraordinary fashion by angels, brought into the world by the extraordinary means of immaculate conception, but then visited by the very ordinary shepherds, does raise the question—what child is this?

The same child who was born "helpless and hungry, lowly, afraid, Wrapped in the chill of midwinter [who] comes now among us born into poverty's embrace." What child is this? In a mashup of these two carols, we find the answer:

"Who is this who lives with the lowly, sharing their sorrows, knowing their hunger?"

"This, this, is Christ the King whom shepherds guard and angels sing!"[12]

"What child is this who, laid to rest, on Mary's lap is sleeping? Whom angels greet with anthems sweet, while shepherds watch are keeping?"

"This is Christ, revealed to the world in the eyes of a child, a child of the poor."[13]

A child of the poor—the poor in spirit, the lonely, the angry, the heartbroken, the despairing; all those suffering in body, mind, or spirit. Jesus knows what all of that is like. He understands life's hardships, "sharing [our] sorrows, knowing [our] hunger," precisely because he lived as one of us, obscure for most of his life.

In all those years as Jesus grew up from a baby to an adult, he experienced life just as any human does: knowing hunger, thirst, experiencing anger, heartbreak, despair, fear, and suffering in body, mind, and spirit. And because he knows what it's like to be human, what it's like to be us, he empathizes with us. He meets us in that suffering with comfort and peace, with an arm around our shoulders and an encouraging word to say to us. Paul puts it well in Hebrews: We have a high priest who can sympathize with us. (Hebrews 4:15)

Jesus, the extraordinary coming of God in human form, Emmanuel, God with us, comes into the world through a rather ordinary birth, born to the most ordinary of parents who live in an obscure, backwater Galilean town, greeted by the most ordinary people imaginable; a child of the poor who grew up knowing what it's like to be poor in spirit, suffering just as we do.

What child is this? This, this, is Christ the King!

Months after my terrible experience of being lost and afraid that midwinter day, graduate school moved on for me. Continued training as a counselor eventually caused me to awaken to a tough reality: I had no idea how to empathize with others and I was extremely immature in my emotional intelligence. What broke that day was my insular, prideful self that thought it knew everything and could tell everyone how they were supposed to live.

But healing, true healing, didn't come until a Christmas season a couple of years later. It was during Advent that I found healing in my soul, experiencing the power of Jesus's friendship and empathy with my plight. It happened, in large part, because I answered the question, "What child is this?" I said, "This, this, is Christ the King of my life!"

I had struggled to believe that God could heal the broken parts of me. But with the angel Gabriel, I came to believe, "Nothing will be impossible with God" (Luke 1:37). That included my healing. And when I confessed that nothing is impossible for God, and that I needed what only God could provide, I found the healing journey that led me to emotional maturity and a deep well of empathy.

When I confessed who Jesus is in my life, acknowledging that healing can only come from God, I found my way forward through the fog, through the midwinter season of life. Throughout the gospels, Jesus is famous for asking the disciples during his earthly ministry, "Who do you say that I am?" It's the same question as, "What child is this?"

So I invite you to ask yourself: What child is this? Who do you say Jesus is?

As we walk this journey of suffering, answering that question matters. To be on a journey of suffering is to also be on a journey with Jesus, for our faith is inevitably altered by our experience of suffering. Like with so much else we have seen so far, denial is our enemy. We must accept that we need to answer this question, even if the answer is, "I don't know" or "I'm not sure anymore." Honesty in answering the question opens our hearts to walk with Jesus through the land of suffering. Doubt is the fertile soil in which faith grows best. When we answer the question, however we answer it, we will gradually awaken to Jesus's presence with us. When we are "lonely, afraid, wrapped in the chill of midwinter," Jesus "comes now, among us, born into poverty's embrace, giving new life for the world." We must answer the question for ourselves, "What child is this? or, put another way, "Whom do I say Jesus is?"

God came down in human form to be one of us, to empathize with us humans. That's "love's pure light,"[14] as described in "Silent Night": "Silent night, holy night, Son of God, love's pure light, radiant beams from thy holy face with the dawn of redeeming grace, Jesus, Lord, at thy birth, Jesus, Lord, at thy birth." Only love, that unconditional love God has for each of us as God's creation, would cause God to want to find out what life was like for us. Only that kind of amazing, passionate, intense love would cause God to want to suffer as we humans suffer.

In this very ordinary human birth, we see God doing something extraordinary: choosing to be ordinary, just like us, to know what life is like for us, actually choosing to experience suffering, just as we do. We see, ultimately, how God was and is truly with us, Emmanuel. We see an extraordinary love for us ordinary people that we find through the ordinary birth of an extraordinary God; a God who wants to live life with us through all our trials, challenges, temptations, and suffering. As it says in "O Holy Night," "In all our trials born to be our friend."[15]

God with us, Emmanuel, born to us so long ago to be one of us, among us; a child of the poor.

As "Child of the Poor" asks, "Who is this who lives with the lonely, sharing their sorrows, knowing their hunger?" This, this, is Christ the King!

Field Notes

Whom do you say Jesus is?

Chapter 10

Expect Something Good

"See, my servant shall prosper;
he shall be exalted and lifted up
and shall be very high.
Just as there were many who were astonished at him
—so marred was his appearance, beyond human semblance,
and his form beyond that of mortals—
so he shall startle many nations;
kings shall shut their mouths because of him,
for that which had not been told them they shall see,
and that which they had not heard they shall contemplate.
Who has believed what we have heard?
And to whom has the arm of the Lord been revealed?
For he grew up before him like a young plant
and like a root out of dry ground;
he had no form or majesty that we should look at him,
nothing in his appearance that we should desire him.
He was despised and rejected by others;
a man of suffering and acquainted with infirmity,
and as one from whom others hide their faces
he was despised, and we held him of no account."
—Isaiah 52:13-53:3

Throughout these chapters, we have found a theme: acceptance of our suffering condition. This is the road less traveled, the narrow path, the right path. Accepting that we are suffering—that we will continue to suffer, that we have no control to end the suffering, and that such suffering will come with hardship and fear—requires courage and faith. It also requires choice. We have the power to choose to accept our suffering condition or reject it. For any of the practical guides that follow to matter, for us to find our way through the land of suffering, we must make such a choice.

As we wrap up this section, where we have looked at what to expect, we consider the choice before us: Will we accept our suffering or try to reject it? Will we invite the hardship, change, insecurity, and fear of the valley to pull up a chair to the table of our heart, experiencing God's empathy? Or will we fight, wrestle, and deny our suffering, thereby getting stuck in the land of suffering?

I must admit, such writing feels something less than pastoral to me, and yet it belies a pastoral reality: Sometimes the life of faith requires courage, tough choices, and going against our basic human instincts. Suffering is one of those times. I find this to be true in my own life, time and again rejecting impulses to push others away, retreat into myself, live in denial, or forcefully push, trying to control what I cannot. Each time, I have to choose yet again to accept my suffering condition. Therein lies the final reality: We must expect to make this choice for acceptance over and over again as we journey through this land of suffering, until one surprising day, we find ourselves on the other side.

So as we wrap up this section on what to expect in the land of suffering, let us consider the plight of George Washington. A few years ago, a friend convinced me to train for a half marathon. Turns out, this tested our friendship. I like running for about two or three miles at a time. I discovered, as I stubbornly trained, that half marathons are not for me. The running became monotonous, and I discovered new parts of my body through pain, but I kept trying for a while, using audiobooks to distract me.

Such was the case for a particular biography of Washington.[16] The author opens with several lists, such as animals Washington owned, titles he had, offices he held. Among the lists are diseases Washington contracted. I could not believe my ears as I listened. He was sick most years of his life with one or more grave illnesses like dysentery, tuberculosis, malaria, and smallpox. He suffered mightily from disease.

But as the author notes, often during an outbreak it was Washington who emerged standing again, healthy, with no long-term side effects from the illness—at least, until his final illness of acute bacterial epiglottitis, which took his life at sixty-seven in 1799. While he suffered terribly (and the book goes into detail about the physical ailments of each condition, along with suffering from bloodletting and other primitive medical techniques), Washington emerged resilient and better for his experience, having grown stronger and more resolute as a result.

Suffering can do that: make us stronger as a result of having lived through whatever ails us to tell the tale. It can, but not always. Whether or not suffering makes us stronger and more resilient is all in how we respond to suffering when it comes our way.

We are well acquainted with suffering in this life. We have known it ourselves in various ways. Suffering comes upon all of us who are human. And in Isaiah, we find someone who has suffered mightily.

The prophet tells us this servant of the Lord "shall prosper ... be exalted and lifted up ... be very high" (Isaiah 52:13). This is the same servant who shall have "no form or majesty that we should look at him, nothing in his appearance that we should desire him" (Isaiah 53:2). He is "despised, rejected ... a man of suffering and acquainted with infirmity ..." (Isaiah 53:3). This servant of the Lord, who will prosper, is a man who, upon seeing him, we would look the other way, either feeling pity for him or reviled by his appearance.

In sum, the suffering servant of the Lord is a person despised by the world, sick, marred in physical appearance, who will also be exalted on high, whose sudden rise to great heights will startle, surprise, the kings of the world. What are we to make of this?

We have perhaps not suffered as mightily as this suffering servant, but we are acquainted with at least some of his suffering. We have known what it is to feel marred physically. For example, I remember back in high school being ashamed of how I looked. Perhaps you have known the kind of body shaming we do to ourselves.

We have also known what it is to be despised. For example, I once worked for a company where I was despised by the president, who sought my ouster and attempted to mar my reputation. Perhaps you have known a time where your reputation was poor, where people at church or in town looked away from you, not wanting to be associated with you.

We have known what it is to be sick, even constantly sick, like Washington much of his life. Certainly, as I write today, I relate strongly here. We are well acquainted with suffering. We know loss and heartache, we know pain and exhaustion, we know despair and hatred. We bump into these things all the time as we live our lives, reminded of relationships lost, family strife, the struggle to pay bills or get out of debt, the fear of what will happen in the future, and the loneliness and depression that cling too closely.

Some suffering, ours or a loved one's, has led us to read this book, as we look for a guide to our journey through the land of suffering. And those things we suffer through can come to feel like a heavy burden, a weight we must carry around with us. Sometimes, with the weights we carry, it feels as though there will never be an end. In fact, it can feel like the suffering is the end, and it will just be that way forever. In the darkness of human suffering, it can seem like there is no end, that the darkness has overwhelmed and it will never be light again. At least, not for us. It might be for other people, but not for us.

Sometimes, suffering is like that, as we have seen in previous chapters. With its fear, it can cause blindness and distort our outlook.

Sometimes, with the weights we carry, we wrestle to seize control of it, to resolve it, to fix it. We're busy trying to make things right again in relationships, trying to fix our illnesses, trying to repair our reputation, trying to get out of our lonely place, trying to make our anger better by acting on it, trying to just end the suffering somehow under our own power. Insecurity, as we saw in Chapter 5, can do that—drive us to try to control what we cannot.

We despair or we wrestle against the weights we carry, against the suffering. That's the typical human response. Sometimes, we're the suffering servant.

We Christians think of the suffering servant as referring to Jesus. In fact, the New Testament quotes parts of this passage when making reference to Christ. He was despised by the world, rejected, marred in appearance, and people thought nothing of him when he went to be crucified. Except for this passage's reference to illness, Jesus fits the bill as the suffering servant of the Lord, fulfilling God's will to defeat sin and death, destroying their power forever.

Not only does Jesus fit what's listed here, but he also surprises the world. Our scripture notes that the kings of the world will be shocked by what they have seen, by what God will do through this suffering servant. It will be unbelievable that a man of no regard—rejected by the world, beaten and bruised, led to his death by a world that rejected him—would be the one whom God prospers, through whom God accomplishes the defeat of sin and death, establishing this man of no regard as the one of highest regard.

Jesus is the suffering servant. And indeed, he suffered mightily. Not just at the crucifixion, either. In each gospel, as the narrative moves inevitably toward the crucifixion, Jesus is increasingly rejected, despised, and alone. Each gospel near the start paints scenes of crowds gathered to hear this new teacher, to be in awe at his powerful works of healing and other miracles. But gradually, the crowds disperse. Jesus becomes increasingly despised, rejected, a persona non grata. By the end, at the crucifixion, Jesus is nearly alone as most of the disciples abandon Jesus.

Only John and the three Marys remain at the foot of the cross until the end.

Jesus suffered mightily physically, spiritually, and socially. In the garden, as the end approached, he prayed that the cup might be taken from him, that he might be spared what's coming. Even Jesus knew despair and fear, knew tremendous suffering as he prayed God might relieve him of it. Then, on the way to Golgotha, he collapsed under the weight of his cross, having to have someone else carry it. Jesus knew the physical, total exhaustion and pain that are sometimes the hallmark of suffering.

But note that for all the ways Jesus shows us his humanity by suffering, he also shows us something else: patience in the suffering. Jesus doesn't wrestle with the weight he carries. He asks God to remove it, but then he asks God that God's will be done. He's not trying to fix things himself; he's not trying to shed the weight on his own. He could have run away, or he could have killed the soldiers who came to arrest him, but he doesn't. He continues to walk forward into a future he knows is filled with hardship. He accepts what's in front of him, the road of suffering, patiently enduring the suffering until it's over.

And that's the example for us as we walk our own journeys. When suffering comes our way, when we know a painful road, when we are despised and rejected, when we feel of low estate, our job is to accept that suffering sometimes happens in this life. We are to continue to walk forward, not trying to fix it ourselves, for we cannot; not trying to escape the suffering, for we cannot; instead walking forward, just as Jesus shows us.

Jesus walks forward into his suffering, accepting it. He can do so because he has hope: God will redeem his suffering, turning what was meant for evil into a powerful good.

So it is for us.

The promise of being one of God's people is that suffering is not forever; God will do something new and surprising through our suffering, turning it into a powerful good. That is God's will. That is what we call redemption, and it can always capstone our suffering.

God redeems our suffering, taking what we go through and making us stronger as a result.

And the best way to see that is to look back to the past. Philip

Yancey, the Christian author, says that "faith is believing in advance what will only make sense in reverse."[17] To have that kind of faith, we must look back to our past to see where God has provided, knowing that God will do it again.

So think back to past suffering you've known, ways that you've experienced tremendous hardship in this life. Can you see where God has taken the difficult, terrible things in your life and made something wonderful out of it? Something good? Something that's used for the benefit of others?

I have known those who suffered through cancer and beat it who are now the best encouragers to those suffering under a recent cancer diagnosis. I have known and seen those who have experienced tragic deaths be the best comforters of those who recently experienced a tragic death in their own life. I have known how those who once felt their reputations were ruined and then restored help others find their way. This, in fact, is part of the design of addiction support groups like AA and Al-Anon: Those who are further down the journey of sobriety are there to help those just starting, sharing how God redeemed their addiction and providing strength for those wrestling mightily against their own addiction.

God takes the suffering we've known and makes something good out of it, something powerful, something so amazing that it's astonishing to those who knew us when we were suffering, who knew what we went through.

How do we wait through suffering, even when things are at their bleakest? We wait in the hope of knowing God is going to do something amazing, something surprising, with our suffering, turning our suffering into a gift we can give to the world. We believe in advance what will only make sense in reverse.

That, in fact, is God's will. Sometimes, God allows suffering to happen in our lives. Other times, it's just the consequence of the presence of evil in the world. But regardless, God does something new and amazing in our lives, something incredible, something surprising, through our suffering by redeeming it, giving us a gift to give to others who are suffering as we once did.

God will do this. That is, if we will let him.

While we have known people who suffered and came out resilient, equipped to help others, we have also known people who suffered and never seemed to have emerged from the suffering. After a period of time since the suffering began, they have become bitter, resentful, rejecting of help, isolated, hateful, despising, and angry. They know little of God's redemption; they are stuck in their suffering and the hardened, negative emotions that go with it.

The difference between those stuck in their suffering and those who know God's redemption is just this: Do we, in the midst of suffering, become hopeless, believing that it's the end, or do we accept that there will be suffering in our lives, choosing to wait through it, patiently enduring, believing that God will redeem it in the end?

The latter is the example Jesus shows us: accepting that suffering will happen in our lives. It's inevitable; we cannot avoid it. Typically, there's little we can do while we're suffering. After we've visited the doctor, taken the medicine, apologized to those we've hurt or offended, confessed our sins, admitted we're powerless to change things, done what it is in our power to do, the task of suffering is to accept our suffering, to embrace it even, patiently enduring it.

And we can do so if we believe, if we cling to the belief, that God will do something good through our suffering. That's how we become the resilient people of God. We accept our human limitations to end the suffering and we reject the temptation to believe there's no hope for us. Those who do the opposite, believing there is no hope or trying to fix their suffering under their own power, get stuck in their suffering, becoming bitter, angry, and isolated.

This is the paradoxical reality of our suffering. When we try to fix it ourselves, we get stuck in our suffering and it is never resolved. When we accept that suffering will happen and rely on God alone to fix it, to redeem it, to bring us out of it, we find that one day our suffering does end and God has done a powerful work of redemption in our lives.

Resilience in this life comes by placing our hope for resolution of our suffering in God's hands, not our own.

In the introduction, I noted that too often, Christian teaching on suffering speaks only of a future hope without providing any guidance for journeying through the present. Here, we look to the future to help us on the journey because we must walk through the land of suffering with the end in mind. If we stop believing that we will get out of the land of suffering, if we fail to have any hope for the future, we will get stuck, wandering aimlessly, growing more tired and eventually resentful, bitter, and angry. That said, we also cannot focus exclusively on the future, having no tools nor resources to journey through our suffering. We must balance the two, looking toward a future filled with hope and grabbing at resources for the present.

Quite often in my own journey, I have had to rekindle my hope. Despair comes in waves, with some days harder than others. To admit I am despairing is to begin the journey to acceptance. Then, having accepted my despairing condition, I ready myself for God to rekindle my hope.

Such came through in the writing of this book. I placed a phone call to a friend, seeking to check on him as he navigates leadership challenges. After talking for a while, he asked how I was doing. Almost unconsciously, I started dumping, venting, and in the end it was clear that I was despairing, having little hope. He responded graciously and then suggested I write this book—that voice of God in a southern drawl from the introduction. Suddenly, I knew God was calling me to do just that. I became excited, eager. I started to have many ideas. I had hope again.

So I write this book, I labor, as a present-focused way to journey through suffering. I do so with hope: that I will emerge from this valley back to the mountaintop and that you, dear reader, will be helped.

Our suffering in this life does not have the final word. God will do something new and surprising through us, giving us a gift to give to those who know our same suffering. If only we will, while we're suffering, patiently accept our suffering, clinging to the hope by believing in advance what will only make sense in reverse. If God has done it before, God will do it again.

That's how we emerge resilient from suffering in this life, better even for the experience, having grown stronger as a result. Suffering can do that: make us stronger as a result of having lived through whatever ails us to tell the tale, just like George Washington and all his illnesses. Suffering can do that because God does that. God will take our suffering and turn it to good. God will do so because our suffering, once redeemed by God, will become a gift to the world. We will become the people who can comfort like no other, can offer encouragement like no other, can pray like no other, helping and healing those who are suffering as we once did.

Accept your suffering in the hope that God will do something wonderfully surprising through it, giving you a gift to give to the world. God will redeem our suffering. Then we will be the resilient people of God.

Field Notes

What do you need to do today to embrace your suffering, accepting your journey through the land of suffering?

Part 2

Survival Strategies

I heard the bells on Christmas Day
Their old, familiar carols play,
And wild and sweet
the words repeat
Of peace on earth, good-will to men.

And thought how, as the day had come,
The belfries of all Christendom
Had rolled along
The unbroken song
Of peace on earth, good-will to men!

Till, ringing, singing on its way,
The world revolved from night to day,
A voice, a chime
A chance sublime
Of peace on earth, good-will to men!

Then from each black, accursed mouth
The cannon thundered in the South,
And with the sound
The carols drowned
Of peace on earth, good-will to men!

It was as if an earthquake rent
The hearth-stones of a continent
And made forlorn
The households born
Of peace on earth, good-will to men!

And in despair I bowed my head;
"There is no peace on earth," I said;
"For hate is strong,
And mocks the song
Of peace on earth, good-will to men!"

Then pealed the bells more loud and deep:
"God is not dead, nor doth He sleep!
The Wrong shall fail,
The Right prevail,
With peace on earth, good-will to men!"

—Henry Wadsworth Longfellow

Chapter 11

Lean on Friends

"Then I saw that all toil and all skill in work come from one person's envy of another. This also is vanity and a chasing after wind. Fools fold their hands and consume their own flesh. Better is a handful with quiet than two handfuls with toil and a chasing after wind. Again, I saw vanity under the sun: the case of solitary individuals, without sons or brothers; yet there is no end to all their toil, and their eyes are never satisfied with riches. 'For whom am I toiling,' they ask, 'and depriving myself of pleasure?' This also is vanity and an unhappy business.

Two are better than one because they have a good reward for their toil. For if they fall, one will lift up the other, but woe to one who is alone and falls and does not have another to help. Again, if two lie together, they keep warm, but how can one keep warm alone? And though one might prevail against another, two will withstand one. A threefold cord is not quickly broken."
—*Ecclesiastes 4:4-12*

MONDAY NIGHT AT THE HOSPITAL, in December 2023, was the lowest point of my current journey of illness. We received tremendous care from the hospitalist there, whose wife is friends with Dana from back when we all lived in Eastman, Georgia. Po, the hospitalist, had been reviewing my case from when I went to the ER on the Friday before, giving us advice, asking good questions. When we arrived at the hospital Sunday, he had a battery of tests all lined up. I was quickly ushered to a room, where Po came to ask a series of questions, digging deeper into what was wrong. While he did, a phlebotomist took more blood out of me than I knew I had in me. Good thing I'm not squeamish.

After they'd left, someone came to transport me for a test. I didn't have long to rest before another test was done. And another. And another.

Po kept us up to date, texting Dana results or coming by the room. We knew what was going on, what he was investigating, and what he had ruled out. It was incredible care. Indeed, with Po we saw where "two are better than one."

On Monday evening, he texted Dana with the result of an echocardiogram. I had minor heart failure. We already knew other organs, like my liver, spleen, and kidneys, weren't functioning normally. CT scans showed my spleen and liver were enlarged. Somehow, I was more OK with those organs having issues than my heart. We sat with this news. One of my first thoughts was, "This is how pneumonia kills people." That may have been an overreaction medically, but my head went there, to that place of fear, just as we know to expect when in the land of suffering.

Lying in my bed, holding Dana's hand, I felt very alone.

It wasn't the first time I'd felt very alone while sick, nor the last. Since late September, I'd basically hidden how badly I was feeling much of the time. Some church members and colleagues saw it as I went along, asking how I was doing, and I often replied the way I was talking to myself, downplaying just how bad I felt.

In late September, I got COVID. At least, I'm pretty sure that's what it was. But whatever it was, it left me with lingering congestion and a cough. I also grew increasingly run-down. It was easy for me to blame it on stressors in my life. As you may recall from an earlier chapter, one of our friends had recently died of cancer. We'd buried her days before I got sick. Dana was still recovering from surgery, a recovery that had proved more difficult than expected and taken a toll on the whole family. So I chalked my run-down, congested feeling up to stress. I, of course, talked to Dana about my struggles, for she is incredible support and we have a marriage that daily reminds me how blessed I am by her. Otherwise, though, I remained solitary in my struggles.

Toward the end of October, I'd gotten bad enough to seek help. I did virtual care. They gave me an antibiotic and a steroid. I took them. They made me a little better. But I was still struggling. And again, I could look to my environment and blame that for my struggles. I told myself that life was increasingly stressful for a variety of reasons, laying blame for my condition there. I decided if I managed my stress better, I'd improve. But I remained solitary in my struggles.

Early in November, I learned my dad had serious heart issues. Quickly, they put in a stint. The procedure and further examination revealed he'd had a heart attack, and if they hadn't caught it when they did, he would have probably had a very significant heart attack in the near future. It was hard news. I flew up to Pennsylvania to visit Dad in the hospital, helping Mom out, on a Friday. I flew back late Saturday, after only about twenty-four hours, and came to do church and then a church retreat. That retreat went off the rails, adding to my stress. Again, I blamed stress for how I was feeling. I told almost no one about any of this: how I felt, about my dad, none of it. And certainly, I didn't mention that I was still suffering physically, now often coughing up mucus. I remained solitary in my struggles.

I recall meeting with a dear friend and mentor around this time. In the course of the conversation, I told her how much I had been suffering and how much of a struggle it had been over the past few months. She rightly chided me for not telling her sooner, not seeking her support. She is part of my support system, after all. Her words struck a chord, but I remained solitary in my struggles.

A day or two after the church retreat, I got much sicker, probably from something I picked up on the plane. Whatever it was, congestion got severe and coughing got worse. I'd go for half-mile walks with Quill, our dog, and would have to stop multiple times because I'd be hacking. I started to experience shortness of breath and was really tired. Again, I thought it would pass. Again, I downplayed my symptoms. Again, I said I knew how to take care of myself and I'd do what my friend and former asthma doctor had taught me to do and eventually get better. I remained solitary in my struggles.

After leading an Interfaith Thanksgiving Service, I felt terrible, but I carried on. The following Sunday, I felt awful, but I carried on. Over Thanksgiving, I felt even worse, but I carried on. I preached the next Sunday, feeling not only terrible but also very weak, but I remained solitary in my struggles.

The next day, November 27, 2023, I had to stop. My body was screaming at me. I did virtual care again. More antibiotics. More steroids. I went home. By the end of the week, my congestion was better, but I was very short of breath, very fatigued, and still coughing. I went back to work anyway, still downplaying my condition, remaining solitary.

Staff meeting at church on December 5, 2023, stands out in my memory. It was my first day back in the office and I barely made it in time for the 10:30 a.m. meeting. As we went through the agenda, I found I couldn't focus on what anyone was saying. I was confused. I was struggling to follow along. I felt incredibly weak. Eventually, I couldn't keep going and told everyone I was going home. I stumbled getting up from my chair because I was so weak. I drove home and couldn't keep the road ahead of me in focus. In hindsight, I shouldn't have driven. I got home and collapsed into the bed.

Something was very wrong. And I had, for more than two months, downplayed it. I told myself it was stress, and if I better managed my stress, it would go away. When I managed my stress better and yet got worse, I told myself I would just have to take better care of myself physically, taking more time for rest, and I would get better. When that failed, I still told myself I could handle it. I told myself I didn't need help. I told myself I'd figure it out. I told myself I had it under control. Looking back now, I can see how that was utter foolishness, but at the time, I remained solitary in my struggles.

Qoheleth, the name we use to refer to the author of Ecclesiastes, has something to say to me, and to any of us who can tend to live such solitary lives. It's utter foolishness, as he points out in verse 5. He calls such self-reliant, solitary living "vanity," a chasing after the wind, a famous phrase from throughout the book. He says, "There is no end to all [the toil of solitary individuals]" (Ecclesiastes 4:8), which leaves them unhappy, foolishly consuming their own flesh. I should have told others how I was feeling. I should have reached out for support. I should have stopped working sooner and seen actual doctors, not virtual care. I should not have remained solitary in my struggles.

But work called. Duty called. And to be frank, I was embarrassed. I've always been kind of sickly. Under my former asthma doctor's excellent care, I got sick less often but, over the last few years, when I've gotten sick, it's been really bad. So I get embarrassed having to take sick leave, admitting I don't feel well, because I think I should be like the average person around me. But I've come to realize I'm not the average person. Asthma makes me more prone to get sick and makes those respiratory illnesses worse. I felt sick more days than not and had gotten so used to sinus infections and bronchitis that I could work through them, as I did in November. I know now I have to be more careful with my asthma, an asthma I think has gotten worse. And I know now that I have primary immunodeficiency, which as I write requires that I act like it's the pandemic all over again: masking in public, avoiding crowds, while also closely watching my diet, all while I deal with chronic fatigue and wait for insurance to approve the necessary treatment.

But how many of us are like me and keep working when hardship comes? How many of us just keep going? How many of us hear a voice in our heads telling us to just keep going? We don't tell others about our suffering. We don't share when we're struggling. We don't reach out for help. We think, "This is going to get better, I'm OK, I don't need help, I can figure this out on my own, others might think worse of me if I talk about how I'm struggling, my reputation might get impinged," and other self-talk that keeps us living as solitary individuals through our struggles, whether physical, emotional, or spiritual. That's what I was doing all through the fall with my physical condition.

And to us, us solitary, self-reliant, individuals, Qoheleth says, this is foolishness, vanity, a chasing after the wind. an unhappy business.

Why do we deprive ourselves of pleasure by living such solitary, self-reliant lives? Why do we engage in this unhappy business, consuming our own flesh as we fold our hands, resigned that we must for some reason remain solitary in our struggles. Why do we keep toiling away when our bodies, our minds, our hearts, and our souls tell us we need to stop?

I had to face those questions myself.

The day after I announced my leave, I received several text messages of support, but one in particular stood out. My mother-in-law, Lynette, texted me this: "I'm sorry that you are having to go through all of this. I know how hard it is to explain to others when you have a hard time understanding yourself. Longing to be well. Wanting to be the you that was. This won't last forever." That was very kind, but then she said this: "God and so many of the people you've touched through the years are on your side and are ready to help take this burden from you. We all love you!"

She was prophetic. So many people in my life reached out to me to offer support. The response was overwhelming. I heard from people I hadn't heard from in years. I received the most touching messages. And I realized I wasn't going through this alone, I didn't need to be embarrassed, and I certainly didn't need to remain solitary in my struggles.

So I started keeping up with my friends and family. As I worsened over the coming days, Dana and I kept them close. When I saw my primary care doctor in early December and we tried another round of antibiotics and steroids, we reached out for support. When that treatment failed, and I went from walking my driveway to only being able to walk in the house because of weakness, we reached out for support. When I went to the ENT and he said I had a "raging sinus infection," we reached out for support. When I went to the ER the next day with chest pain, we kept our friends and family posted on all the developments and on our deep frustrations with the care we were receiving. We reached out for support.

Then on Sunday, December 17, 2023, I woke up and walked around the corner to our bathroom and nearly fell down. I had to lean on the counter for support. I was so weak that I couldn't stand without assistance.

That was the day I got admitted to the hospital. Dana started calling medical friends, working on figuring out what to do. I started texting friends and family, reaching out for support.

And that next evening, feeling alone with the news that I had minor heart failure, we quickly decided to reach out again to our friends and family for support. I initially resisted that. A habit of living too solitary a life remained within me. But I ceded my self-reliant position, recognizing I needed support in this darkest hour of my ailment.

We sat down and texted a thread called S3, my close-knit clergy group and their spouses that functions like a small group. We texted a group thread called Councilman and Friends, composed of dear friends, one of whom had recently won election to the Eastman City Council. We texted The Village, named for an area of dorms at James Madison University, where we met two lifelong and dear friends. We texted Highland Terrace, another thread with our friends who are more like family, named for the street we all used to live on when we first became friends. We texted my spiritual director. We texted my parents, Dana's parents, my brother and sister-in-law, my mentor, my former asthma doctor, and my staff who are now dear friends. No one, of course, had any answers, but much support arrived as our phones lit up with messages.

Throughout my forty-eight hours in the hospital, people stopped by. I'll never forget a knock on the door and a dear friend from Eastman popping his head around the door. We had not spoken in a while, custom when a Methodist pastor moves, but he had kept up with me and knew of my suffering. And there he was, talking with me at my bedside, laughing together like old times. Our faces lit up, joy ushered into the room, and we found the grace that is the presence of Christ "where two or three are gathered" (Matthew 18:20).

And in it all I saw Qoheleth's wisdom: "Two are better than one … if they fall, one will lift up the other … " (Ecclesiastes 4:9-10).

How ironic it is that I, a pastor who has spent a career lifting others up, was so reticent to let others lift me up. But I suspect I'm not alone in that. Many of us, pastors or not, are much more comfortable with the idea of lifting others up than allowing others to lift us up. There's a humility required to allow others to lift us up, to admit we're struggling, to come out of our solitary lives. Human nature, it seems, tends toward solitary living, lying to us that we're self-reliant. That's part of our broken human nature. It's true for all of us. And to come out and humbly ask for help when struggling in body, mind, or spirit is uncomfortable. Humility and going against our human nature are always uncomfortable.

But it's so necessary. People have asked me how I got through. How I am making it through this terrible bout of illness. My answer is the love and support I felt from all my friends, family, and members of churches I have served, which is itself a mirror reflection of the love and support of God. And that makes all the difference. Once I reached out for support after Lynette texted me on December 7, I rarely wavered in hope. My emotional and spiritual health was good. My attitude stayed rather sunny. I had hard moments, like finding out I had mild heart failure, but most of the time, I was hopeful.

That hope has persisted, despite setbacks. Insurance approval for treatment took longer than expected. As I waited anxiously, I texted and reached out to friends and family. When the committee at Mulberry voted me out, I reached out to my support network. There, especially, I saw this principle at play. Many members of Mulberry reached out to me, hurting themselves, bewildered by the decision of the church, but wanting to be of comfort and support to me and my family. Two are, indeed, better than one.

In the end, I had two strains of antibiotic-resistant bacteria in my sinuses, or basically dual sinus infections, that'd I'd been carrying since early October. This explained why the oral antibiotics I took throughout the fall were only partially effective. I required intravenous antibiotics to defeat these two strains, but we didn't know that until I was in the hospital in mid-December. Those strains migrated to my chest in November, probably aided by whatever I had picked up on the plane back from Pennsylvania, leading to bronchitis the week before Thanksgiving. I now can see that I did the Interfaith Thanksgiving Service and led worship services in November with bronchitis and maybe already having developed pneumonia. By the time I got back from celebrating Thanksgiving, I definitely had pneumonia. By the time I got to the hospital, I had all this plus I'd also picked up RSV, which with my asthma is a very challenging illness, and most likely also had mono.

The combination of infections, along with all the medicines I'd been taking, had also impacted my organ function. Of course, my asthma made all of those things worse, as if they weren't enough on their own. Primary immunodeficiency is the answer to how I got so sick, but determining that, and beginning treatment, took six months from the point I entered the hospital.

I still have a long way to go. Now I know I have had this primary immunodeficiency all my life, and it explains so much of my medical history. I eagerly anticipate the treatment. Research sent to me by my new asthma doctor shows tremendous and hopeful outcomes for those receiving treatment. But there are still many hard days, just like the day I realized I should write this book. And on those days, I again reach out for support.

The longer this time of suffering has lasted, the more I worry that I have exhausted the sympathy of my friends and family. This time of suffering has now gone on for several months, with many ups and downs. When I have another downturn and I reach for my phone to send a text to these friends and family, or when we post to social media, I worry I will find I have exhausted sympathy. And yet, time and again, I find that no sympathy is exhausted, people still care, and they are generous with their sympathy. I find grace, hope, and God's very presence in this reality.

Whatever's in front of me as I walk this journey, I don't do so alone. I walk the journey with my friends. I walk the journey with my family. I will not live such a solitary life again. I will let people in sooner. I will talk more about my struggles. I will take better care of myself by not living a solitary, self-reliant lifestyle.

Our human nature tends us toward solitary living. We tend, like me, to downplay our struggles and not reach out for support. But my experience has shown me the wisdom of Qoheleth's words: Two are definitely better than one.

God created us for companionship. When God created Adam, God declared it was not good for him to be alone, and created Eve. When God called Moses, he also called Aaron and Miriam to be supports for him. When God called David, he gave him a close friend in Jonathan who saw him through David's hardships. When Mary received the news she was pregnant, the angel sent her to her cousin Elizabeth, for both of them to not be alone in their remarkable journeys. When Jesus sent the disciples into villages, he sent them two by two. And later, when Jesus commends prayer, he notes, "Where two are three are gathered, there I am with them." In Acts, the first thing the disciples do after Jesus ascends is to select a replacement for Judas. When they begin their ministries, they form communities of support. Even Paul, whom we often discuss as an individual, always had fellow travelers with him and always had other apostles to whom he could turn. Two are better than one.

And then, three are even better. Note that the scripture follows this pattern: one, two, three. Qoheleth condemns solitary living, declares that two are better than one, and then finishes with a famous verse, "A threefold cord is not quickly broken" (Ecclesiastes 4:12). When we choose to live life with others, when we reach out for support, when we ask for help, when we confess our struggles, when we do the uncomfortable thing and choose humility to say we cannot do it alone, we find the support and love of our friends. And in that support and love, we experience God's support and love. That's the third cord. God is with us in the community we build with our friends and family. God's love comes through. God is present. The love and support of our friends is a mirror reflection of God's love and support. The support and love of friends brings with it the support and love of God. Indeed, a threefold cord is not quickly broken.

I wonder: Who are the people in your life who give you support? Through whom do you experience the love and support of God when you reach out with your struggles? This is the primary thing Sunday school classes and small groups provide. It's the primary thing families are built for, and we as families learn how to give each other support at church. That's because God designed the church to support one another during hardship.

I also wonder, when struggles come and life gets hard, do you reach out for support? Or are you like I was, telling yourself you can figure it out, you can make it work, you don't need help, it's too embarrassing to ask for anyway and you'll just double down on yourself? That is an unhappy business. It leads to consuming our own flesh, literally cannibalizing ourselves, as we eat away from the inside out because we won't ask for help. Whatever your struggles in body, mind, or spirit, God made us to bear those burdens with others, to share together in the journey, for when we do so, we experience the love and support of God.

Lying in that hospital bed on that Monday, Dana reached over from her chair and said, "You need to check your email." There, among all the junk emails we all get, was a surprising, deeply moving, gift. The music director at Mulberry, Terre Johnson, had composed a hymn for me.[18] We all process hardships in our own ways, and Terre explained in the body of the email that his way of processing his empathy for me, and of sharing his love for me, was to write me a hymn. I read it over and over again.

In that hymn was God's love and support, brought through in powerful fashion by the love and support of a friend. Two are better than one. A threefold cord is not quickly broken. God's love and support comes through when we share life together with friends and family.

We need each other. We were not meant to live solitary lives. We must give up the solitary, self-reliant lifestyles of deciding we can do it on our own, that we don't need help, that it's too embarrassing to reach out for help, that we can figure things out on our own. I have learned that such is vanity, a chasing after the wind, and leads to consuming myself.

We need friends. We need family. We need church. We were built for them. God made us for them. And through them, we experience the love and support of God.

Whenever hardship comes, reach out for help from friends, family, and the church. There, you will meet the love and support of God. Indeed, two are better than one, and a threefold cord is not quickly broken.

Field Notes

Name your support system. As you suffer, when have you last reached out to them for support?

Chapter 12

Be a Friend

*"And Mary said,
'My soul magnifies the Lord,
and my spirit rejoices in God my Savior,
for he has looked with favor on the lowly state of his servant.
Surely from now on all generations will call me blessed,
for the Mighty One has done great things for me,
and holy is his name;
indeed, his mercy is for those who fear him
from generation to generation.
He has shown strength with his arm;
he has scattered the proud in the imagination of their hearts.
He has brought down the powerful from their thrones
and lifted up the lowly;
he has filled the hungry with good things
and sent the rich away empty.
He has come to the aid of his child Israel,
in remembrance of his mercy,
according to the promise he made to our ancestors,
to Abraham and to his descendants forever.'"*
—Luke 1:46-55, *The Magnificat*

A THRILL OF HOPE, the weary world rejoices.
Christina Rossetti sat at her home. This English poet of moderate

fame had published many poems before in her life, mostly focused on things that would gain readership. But now, having been diagnosed with Graves' disease and having suffered a near-fatal heart attack, she found herself convalescing in a dark season of life, a season that gave rise to new poetry, one we examined briefly in Chapter 3.

As she struggled with her health, it's understandable that the first words to her poem would be, "In the bleak midwinter, frosty wind made moan, earth stood hard as iron, water like a stone."[19] She paints a stark picture of the bleakness of the middle of winter.

Rossetti wrote during the Advent season to process her emotions after her diagnosis and come to grips with her new reality. Friends encouraged her to turn to her favorite medium, poetry, as a means of coping. And as she writes during an Advent season, she imagines that same midwinter scene surrounding the birth of Jesus. In the midst of the cold and hardness of winter, the warmth and gentleness of a savior is born. In the harshness of the season, God's graciousness comes into being. Her study in contrasts is her way of saying, "Come, thou long expected Jesus!"[20]

It may sound odd to make such a request when Jesus has come into the world already. And yet, there's power in asking Jesus to come again, for I don't know about you, but sometimes I need a fresh outpouring of Christ in my life, especially when navigating suffering. In her midwinter season, Rossetti needed that as well.

That prayer, "Come, thou long expected Jesus," gets full voice in Charles Wesley's hymn. Wesley declares:

> Come, thou long-expected Jesus,
> born to set thy people free;
> from our fears and sins release us,
> let us find our rest in thee.
> Israel's strength and consolation,
> hope of all the earth thou art;
> dear desire of every nation,
> joy of every longing heart.[21]

Sometimes, we all need to experience a fresh outpouring of just what Wesley describes: to be set free, to find release from our fears and sins in our rest in thee. That's especially true in the midwinter seasons of life, as Rossetti poetically declares. Sometimes, we all need:

"A thrill of hope, the weary world rejoices."[22]

Although, we must admit such sentiment was not Mary's first reaction to the news of Jesus in her womb. Like Zechariah, she doubts when the angel gives her the news of her role in bringing Jesus into the world. Unlike Zechariah, she is not made mute but told to go visit her cousin, Elizabeth, Zechariah's wife.

We can imagine Mary, the angel having left, feeling bewildered and overcome. Her? An unwed teenager? The mother of the savior of the world? It would be scandalous! Imagine today finding out about an unwed teen mother you personally know. Now imagine yourself believing her when she tells you she's carrying the savior of the world through an immaculate conception. It's hard to believe now and it was unbelievable back then.

Most of all to Mary. How in the world is this to happen? But she follows the angel's command and travels to see Elizabeth. There, through Elizabeth, she finds all she needs. She gains right and true perspective. She can see what God is doing and she can now grasp it, understand it, and even sing it.

And so, because of her visit to Elizabeth, she's able to declare in her song, "The Magnificat," that God's mercy is coming afresh and anew, that God will scatter the proud, remove the lofty from their thrones, and lift up the lowly. God will fill the hungry and keep promises of old. Above all, God will deliver the people from what ails them. God will deliver them from their midwinter season: their cold, harsh, and hard time in history.

God will deliver. God will bless.

And Mary realizes all this through visiting with Elizabeth. From that friendship with her cousin, she is able to do what she could not before; it's the same thing Rossetti found the strength to do through her poem because of the encouragement of her friends:

She can give God what she has; give God her heart.

"A thrill of hope, the weary world rejoices."

Edmund Sears was a failed priest. At least, he thought he was, as he struggled through a midwinter season in his life. He'd had what we United Methodists would call a large appointment—a large church to pastor. But it had broken him. Details of why it had broken him are unclear, but he returned to his Wayland, Massachusetts, home, having broken down. Sears knew a cold, harsh, dark midwinter season in his life as he wrestled with failure, experiencing a season of suffering.

And in his life, feeling crushed and carrying a heavy load, he penned these words:

> And ye, beneath life's crushing load,
> whose forms are bending low,
> who toil along the climbing way
> with painful steps and slow,
> look now! for glad and golden hours
> come swiftly on the wing.
> O rest beside the weary road,
> And hear the angels sing![23]

Somehow, even while broken and overcome, he could look and see that God was still working, God was still moving, and God would deliver him; from his fears and sins Christ would release him, and he would find his rest in thee. Somehow, he knew, just knew, that God would come swiftly on the wing, bringing those glad and golden hours. And so he could rest beside the weary road and hear the angels sing. He once again felt God in his heart. He was free, filled with joy.

His carol, "It Came Upon a Midnight Clear," one he wrote after the encouragement of a friend, demonstrates what Rossetti and Mary knew: that especially in the midwinter seasons of life, when we give God our hearts, we discover:

A thrill of hope, our weary world rejoices.

Sitting in church in France one day in the 1850s, John Sullivan Dwight was feeling dispirited. He was visiting from America, where he worked hard for the abolitionist movement to end slavery. But at the moment of his visit to France, his home country seemed ready to erupt into war. It was not what he hoped for. He was in his own midwinter season of life, his form bending low under the crushing load of what seemed to be a failed movement to end slavery, suffering mightily.

But then, as he sits in church pondering the state of things, a magisterial song breaks out. He hears the words "a thrill of hope, the weary world rejoices," and his weary soul rejoices.

As he traveled home, he took the song with him, translating it into English. When he arrived back in America, he ran straight to his abolitionist friends to share the song he'd learned, but not just the words and music he had learned. He had added a new verse, writing these lines:

> Truly He taught us to love one another;
> His law is Love and His gospel is peace;
> Chains shall He break, for the slave is our brother,
> And in His name all oppression shall cease.
> Sweet hymns of joy in grateful chorus raise we;
> Let all within us praise His holy name![24]

"O Holy Night," with this additional verse, became an instant hit throughout churches in the northern United States. Abolitionists across the country found inspiration in the new verse. Dwight and his friends knew that the slave was their brother, just as we are all brothers and sisters in Christ, and that through their efforts, God would break chains and in his name all oppression would cease. They found encouragement and once again gave God their hearts.

For them, as they gave God their hearts, it was indeed a thrill of hope. Their weary world rejoiced.

We are truly blessed by these Christmas carols, and not just by the carols themselves, but by knowing the backstory. We see how out of life's trials, life's crushing loads, life's oppression, life's dismay and decay, indeed out of the midwinter seasons of life, Christ was born to be our friend in all our trials. Then ever, ever, praise we, because we know that God will deliver us. Mary could see it, too. She saw that, even through her, God would deliver.

In all these stories, for each person to discover that Christ releases us from our fears and sins, finding our rest in thee, all it took to find a thrill of hope so their midwinter season of life could rejoice was to give God their heart, as we saw in Part 1, and some friendship along the way.

Sometimes, we all need a fresh outpouring of Christ into our hearts. Sometimes, our prayer is indeed, "Come, thou long-expected Jesus!" And when we're in that kind of midwinter season; when we feel our forms bending low, with painful steps and slow, the task before is to look now! For glad and golden hours come swiftly on the wing. In those seasons of life, we find the vision we need to see those glad and golden hours on the wing by walking the journey of life with a friend.

When Sears wrote "It Came Upon a Midnight Clear," a friend had encouraged him to write to help find a sense of peace and joy in his brokenness. When Rossetti penned "In the Bleak Midwinter," she was encouraged by friends. When Dwight brought home "O Holy Night," adding his famous verse, he was encouraged by his abolitionist friends. When Mary sang her song of praise, "The Magnificat," she was encouraged by her friend and cousin Elizabeth.

Through the companionship of their friends, they could see the world through fresh eyes, discovering where God was delivering, providing, and upholding. Indeed, they experienced a thrill of hope and they, in their weary worlds, rejoiced because they had found through their friendships that despite their present circumstances, God was Emmanuel—God with us. And then, as Rossetti says, they could give God their hearts, no matter how poor their state.

Friendship along the toiling way helps us find Christ in our midst. Then, we can give God our hearts.

Then we discover that thrill of hope; our weary world rejoices.

Consider Mary, who carried God in her womb. She needed her eyes opened to see beyond the overwhelm and dismay of the angel's pronouncement. She needed to see beyond her fear and doubt. It's easy to think of Mary as this stoic, heroic exemplar of the faith and forget that, at first, she was a frightened teenage girl suddenly thrust into a role she did not ask for, suffering under this news. She found the strength she needed, and gained sight of what God was doing in her life, because of her friend. And with that companionship, she was able to give God her heart.

And that's just the point: To reveal the heart of God and help others give God their heart, one of the best things we can be is a friend.

When we're in the midwinter seasons of life, praying, "Come, thou long-expected Jesus … set me free," facing sufferings of any kind in body, mind, or spirit, one of the best ways to find Christ in the midst of our suffering is through friendship. We must be brave and bold enough to let others know we're suffering, to reach out for friends, just like Rossetti, Sears, Dwight, and most especially Mary, and just like we saw in the previous chapter. We must be willing to show that our lives aren't perfect, for none of ours are. Sometimes, we all need a fresh outpouring of Christ in our lives, and friendship is a powerful way to bring that fresh outpouring of Christ to someone who's facing a midwinter season of life.

We can be a friend ourselves by being available to others who are carrying a crushing load. We can notice when others seem down and offer to listen, to be present. So much of my pastoral care involves me not saying a whole lot. I do much listening, in part because there's great power in just being present. When we're present with someone's suffering, when we're present beneath their crushing load, their forms bending low, we send a powerful message of how much we care. Our presence with the suffering of others brings Christ to our friend who's suffering, and that presence all by itself declares, "Look now! For glad and golden hours come swiftly on the wing! Oh rest beside the weary road and hear the angels sing."

We can be a friend, and in doing so, we are a tremendous blessing to those facing a midwinter season of life. We don't have to have the right words and we don't have to know what to say, except to say that we're there and we're willing to listen and willing to share the burden. That's all. But that's powerful.

Because when we're such a friend as this, we bring Christ. Our friends may be saying, "Come, thou long-expected Jesus, ... from my fears and sins release us, let us find our rest in thee."[25] And when we decide to be a friend, we say back to them, "Look now! For glad and golden hours come swiftly on the wing," "for Christ in all our trials was born to be our friend."

In our friendship, in choosing to be a friend, we bring a thrill of hope so that our friend's weary world can rejoice.

Without friendship like this, the Christmas carol authors we've noted in this chapter would never have penned their words, words that out of their suffering lift up our souls. Words that speak directly to the midwinter seasons of life.

In Chapter 11, we saw the necessity of reaching out to friends for support. Here, even while we are suffering, we see the necessity of being a friend. I have experienced what I can only describe as a mystical reality: that when we care for others, we experience care ourselves. Back in the introduction, I told the story of my friend Graham, who recommended I write this book. I called him in order to be a friend, and in the midst of that call, he was a friend to me. When the church committee voted me out, church members at Mulberry called me to check on me, even though they expressed how much they were hurting. As I have suffered, I have yet reached out when friends are going through their own sufferings, and found there this mystical reality: When we reach out in care, when we are a friend, we receive care ourselves.

That is the sacrificial love of Christ on display. In his life, he sacrificed for us, suffering as we do, learning to walk along the road "with painful steps and slow." Yet, as "O Holy Night" proclaims, "In all our trials, [Jesus was] born to be our friend." When we are a friend to others, no matter how much we are suffering, we bring Christ to that friendship. And when they meet us there, in the land of suffering, together we experience the love and care of our savior.

Friendship, as common as it sounds, makes such a huge difference. We bring Christ to each other when we share in each other's crushing loads. We bring hope and deliverance from what ails us, what makes us know a weary world. Friendship brings a thrill of hope to the midwinter seasons of life because friendship, true friendship, brings Christ to life's crushing loads.

No matter how hard and difficult the road becomes as you journey through the land of suffering, be a friend. Then you both will know a thrill of hope, for your weary worlds will rejoice.

Field Notes

Who in your life needs you to be a friend? How do you imagine being a friend will help you during this time of suffering?

Chapter 13

Practice Examen to Wait Well

"The saying is sure and worthy of full acceptance: that Christ Jesus came into the world to save sinners—of whom I am the foremost. But for that very reason I received mercy, so that in me, as the foremost, Jesus Christ might display the utmost patience as an example to those who would come to believe in him for eternal life."—1 Timothy 1:15-16

How should we wait?

Back in fourth grade, I could not wait for some new Legos to come in the mail. I saved my allowance and birthday money to purchase some specific Legos. They were what I needed for a project I had going on at the time. I was hugely into Legos when I was a boy and played with them all the time. I recalled this memory not long ago when I found a notebook from fourth grade. At the top of many pages, I had written a countdown of how many days until the Legos came in the mail.

As I flipped through the countdown, I discovered something I had forgotten: the Legos were late. They were supposed to take three weeks: an eternity when you're nine years old. Each day past the twenty-first day, I lost more and more patience, writing exasperated things at the top of my page like "when will they come" with a question mark and many exclamation points, growing increasingly hopeless. When they finally did come, I had mixed emotions. I was happy they had finally arrived, but I was also still fuming about how long they had taken. Fair to say, I was not waiting well.

This proved to be a theme in my life, especially recently when awaiting treatment for primary immunodeficiency. But I have learned a few things about how to wait well and how to find hope and promise in the waiting, especially when waiting through suffering.

A few years ago, I went to Green Bough, a prayer retreat center in central Georgia. During a time of listening and prayer with one of the leaders there, I asked this question, "How do you wait well?" noting that I knew I needed to grow in patience. With our future as a family highly uncertain at that time, and many options up in the air, I was finding myself in that pattern just like when I was in fourth grade: growing increasingly agitated and anxious in the waiting such that the waiting itself—or better said, the poor way I was handling the waiting—was preventing me from enjoying the things of life.

Waiting can do that. It's very hard to be patient. How should we wait?

To answer that question, let's consider Paul's faith journey, which is a remarkable one. Born as a Roman citizen to parents of some prosperity, he demonstrated a talent for theology at an early age. He was raised up in the faith to become a pharisee and, upon completing his training, became one of the most zealous of all pharisees. He traveled the region, including Palestine, to encourage fellow Jews to uphold the faith. This gradually included persecuting a brand-new sect of Judaism that also attracted Gentile believers: a sect known at the time as The Way, later to be known as Christianity.

Paul, then named Saul, gained a reputation as one of the most vigilant of the persecutors of Christianity. Famously in the book of Acts, he looks on as Stephen, the first Christian martyr, is stoned, approving of the proceedings. He does so as one of the most zealous proponents of the movement to extinguish this new form of Judaism, which he considered a direct threat to the true form of Judaism the pharisees promoted and enforced.

So here in Timothy, when Paul says that Jesus Christ, through him, showed mercy and "the utmost patience" (1 Timothy 1:16) we can see why. Jesus put up with much persecution, much bad behavior on Paul's part, before finally appearing to him on the Damascus Road, the moment of Paul's conversion. That is tremendous patience on Jesus's part. Many Christians suffered at the hands of Paul and his pharisees. They lived under fear of what these zealous religious leaders would do. Jesus tolerated much suffering on the part of his people, waiting to convert Paul.

This leads us to ask why Jesus waited. Why not convert Paul sooner, save the persecution of these early Christians, and indeed perhaps have saved Stephen's life? Yes, there's tremendous patience shown, especially patience with Paul's behavior. That's what he reports here to Timothy as a way of encouraging Timothy and those who would read this letter: Jesus is patient with you, too. No matter how bad your behavior and no matter for how long, Jesus has patience and will forgive you.

That's a powerful message of grace that leads others to find eternal life in Jesus Christ. It's a beautiful message of divine patience: That no matter what we have done in this life, and no matter for how long, and no matter how much we've wronged God, Jesus has patience with us, forgives us, and receives us into eternal life.

But we're still left with our question: Why did Jesus wait so long to convert Paul? In the waiting, while Jesus showed him the utmost patience, Christians suffered persecution at Paul's hand. Why not convert him sooner?

It's a good question to ask as we learn how to wait well; how to practice patience. And, as we seek an answer to that question, let's also consider another: What are you waiting for?

We're all waiting for something. Sometimes, it's for things to happen, like when I waited for treatment for my condition.

Sometimes, we're waiting for people or circumstances to change: People who do wrong to us, things that harm us, uncomfortable situations, and there's nothing to do but grin and bear it.

Often, we might find ourselves waiting for our suffering to end. We look toward the future, waiting, with growing impatience, for the day that we find our way out of this land of suffering, away from the grief that clings closely, the fear that threatens to consume, the hardship and insecurity we know.

And in the waiting, it's all too easy for that waiting to give way to impatience, marked by being irritable and, often, anxiety. In long-term health issues, in our finances, in family members who continually cause us trouble, in work that never seems to pay off, in so many ways we find ourselves irritable, anxious, stressed, grasping for a sense of control over things while we wait. It's easy to get that way, whether over trivial things like waiting for Legos or more serious things, especially if we're suffering or having to grin and bear it or laboring with no guarantee of anything coming of it. And as our anxiety and irritation grows, impatience can take over our lives, scheming for how we can get things to happen sooner, or end the suffering sooner, or somehow just not have to wait—at least, not wait as long.

Bring to mind when you've had to wait and grown agitated, irritable, totally impatient in the waiting. Maybe there's something right now in your life: waiting for someone to change, waiting for suffering from health or finances to end, waiting for suffering from someone else's bad behavior to end, waiting for your laboring to finally pay off, waiting for the circumstances of your life to change; waiting, impatiently, irritably, anxiously; waiting.

Waiting is hard. And as we grow irritable and anxious, we tend to also grow hopeless: hopeless that the waiting will ever end, hopeless that things will work out. We hear the voice of wisdom in our lives say that good things come to those who wait. But that doesn't make it any easier to wait.

And then, in the waiting, we might ask what's taking God so long to make things right or to bring our waiting to an end. Just like we were asking with Jesus, as to why he didn't convert Paul sooner while Christians suffered, we might ask God why God doesn't act sooner to end our suffering.

How should we wait?

Throughout the Bible, we see God waiting over and over again. In fact, from the very beginning, we see God waiting. When Adam and Eve sin, God says in the garden, "Where are you?" waiting for Adam and Eve to present themselves. In the sinning of the people prior to the flood, God is waiting to see if they would repent. And then, when it's clear they will not, God waits even longer before instructing Noah to build the ark. When the Tower of Babel is being built, God waits a while before destroying the tower and dispersing the people.

God shows patience with Abram and Sarai's lack of faith before they become the Abraham and Sarah of fame. God waits for generations while the people are enslaved in Egypt before acting through Moses to save them. God waits while the people wander in the wilderness, building a golden calf out of their impatience when they decide that God isn't acting the way he should. God is patient with the people once they're in the land as they sin over and over again.

Throughout scripture, God demonstrates patience with the sin of the people time and time again, eventually acting in what the Bible calls "the fullness of time." That phrase shows up again when talking about the arrival of Jesus. A messiah had been promised for generations—at least five hundred years. Scripture says that God sent Jesus "in the fullness of time" (Galatians 4:4), another way of saying at the right time, when God knew things were right.

The scriptural witness shows us that God is patient. God is patient in abiding suffering, for God suffers at the sin of his people and the evil in the world. God is patient in bearing the burdens of his people, especially seen in sending and allowing Jesus Christ to suffer. God is patient in not acting until just the right time, in the fullness of time. And God is patient in continuing to labor, to work, for the good in the world and for the restoration of his people and individuals, just like with Paul.

God is patient. It's not often how we describe God, but there it is, across scripture. God acts at the right time, but of course God was present throughout the times of waiting, too, moving and active.

God does not sit back until the right conditions present themselves. No, in each of these stories and all across scripture, we see God involved, God moving, God acting. Consider, for example, Sarai and Abram. God visits them in person, God sends people their way, God shows up in manifold ways, until finally the time is right and Sarai and Abram become Sarah and Abraham, the father and mother of the people of God.

That holds true for us today. How should we wait? With the knowledge that God is acting and moving in power, now, even if we have not yet realized the end of our waiting. This is good news for us in our waiting. We are not waiting alone, hoping that the timing will soon be right for God to act. God is acting now, moving in power. God is present now, empathizing with our suffering, providing for us.

While we wait for release from suffering, while we look toward the end of our journey in the land of suffering, God is yet active and moving. We may simply not have eyes to see God's actions, blinded as we are by fear, anxiety, hardship, grief, and the like.

To gain eyes to see during this season of waiting through suffering, I recommend a powerful tool. It's a form of Examen, a prayer from St. Ignatius of Loyola, but made simpler, such that anyone, even little children, can use it. To practice this form of Examen, take time either individually or with a close friend or family member and ask these two questions:

What am I most grateful for today?
What am I least grateful for today?[26]

At first, it might feel like it's not doing much. The power of Examen is in daily practice over time. Our family has been practicing this form of Examen many days over dinner for a few years now. In that repetition, we discover where God is active and moving in our lives. Perhaps it's Carter pointing out something wonderful that happened to him that day. Maybe it's Jackson in the midst of a hard day yet still finding something to celebrate. Asking ourselves what we are least grateful for might sound counterintuitive, but quite often, we as a family have found it the more powerful question. Often, one of us will have the same least-grateful thing for several days in a row. Then, one day, we no longer list the particular thing. God has resolved it, and we have gratitude for that resolution as we point out to each other that the former least-grateful item is gone, resolved. God has provided. In this way, we see where God is at work both in the positive and negative things we encounter day to day.

For me, I have discovered I more readily see where God is active and am more positive, especially when I'm suffering, bearing a burden, or otherwise waiting, because this practice of Examen makes me see where God is working, acting, in my life; something I would otherwise miss. It gives me those eyes to see how God is active while I wait.

What am I most grateful for today?

What am I least grateful for today?

Examen helps with the waiting by showing us where God is acting. And that's the answer to how we practice patience now, while we're waiting. We look for where God is acting. Because when we see where God is acting around us, we are reminded that God will act in the things we're waiting for and our waiting will come to an end.

Then we can wait with hope.

Field Notes

What are you most grateful for today? What are you least grateful for today?

CHAPTER 14

Do Things that Bring Joy

"There is a vanity that takes place on earth, that there are righteous people who are treated according to the conduct of the wicked and wicked people who are treated according to the conduct of the righteous. I said that this also is vanity. So I commend enjoyment, for there is nothing better for people under the sun than to eat and drink and enjoy themselves, for this will go with them in their toil through the days of life that God gives them under the sun. When I applied my mind to know wisdom and to see the business that is done on earth, how one's eyes see sleep neither day nor night, then I saw all the work of God, that no one can find out what is happening under the sun. However much they may toil in seeking, they will not find it out; even though those who are wise claim to know, they cannot find it out."—Ecclesiastes 8:14-17

ON A BEAUTIFUL, SUNNY AFTERNOON on a beach vacation a few years ago, I noticed some kids, about twelve, skimboarding. That's where you throw a small surfboard-looking thing out in front of you along the wake and jump on it to slide across the wake. I told Dana it looked like tons of fun and that I should go try it out. She warned me that I'm not twelve and that my center of gravity is much higher and would make skimboarding much harder. I took her call to caution, to accept the limitations of my adult body, as a challenge.

So I ran back to our rental, grabbed the skimboard stored with the beach supplies, and threw it out on the wake. I know when I jumped my feet landed on the board, but only for a split second. My feet went out from under me, over my head, and I hit the hard sand headfirst.

The result was a concussion, which nine days later resulted in post-concussion syndrome, which stuck me in bed in a dark room with no screens for about a week. All because I wanted to have some fun. I should have accepted my limitations.

Vanity. All is vanity.

I think Qoheleth would be amused by our twenty-four-hour news cycle. Qoheleth (pronounced co-helet) is how we refer to the author of Ecclesiastes; it's a word that means teacher in Hebrew and a person history has often thought of as the wise King Solomon. Qoheleth would be amused by the reality that we constantly have, at our fingertips or the end of our remotes, access to all the latest developments in the sagas that grip our attention. I pay attention through listening to the news while driving and through reading the news in the morning. I read widely and with depth to give myself understanding, to be informed.

I want to be informed because I want to feel like I have some sense of understanding, some way of making sense of the world around me. I also deeply believe in the ideal of an enlightened citizenry championed by Thomas Jefferson, among others. Ultimately, I want to feel like I have some control over the world around me through the understanding I gain by staying informed.

Vanity. This also is vanity.

In a moment of significant disappointment in my life, I struggled to accept a new reality, wanting both to understand why it happened and to figure out a way to fix it. Those two things relate well to my personality: I'm a stubborn fixer. If I believe in something, it's going to happen. If there's a way to fix something, I'm going to figure out how to fix it. And if there's understanding to be had, I'm going to understand it. That's my personality. And it can be a tremendous asset and is why I tend to gain a reputation as one who gets things done and as an innovator.

But it's also a liability. I often don't know when to stop. In this particular moment of disappointment, I ran myself ragged trying, with increasing desperation, to understand the disappointment. Why did it happen? Is there a flaw with me? Is there a flaw with the system? Wherever there's a flaw, there must be a solution, so how can I fix it? Can I read this book or go to that conference? Can I find errors in my skillset and then address those errors? Can mentors in my life or trusted counsel point out where I'm needing improvement, whether personally or professionally?

Vanity. This also is vanity.

For me, it's easy to not accept my limits. I want instead to stubbornly say that I am capable and can do it on my own. Historically, I have had a tough time believing there's anything beyond my understanding, whether it's skimboarding, the news, or why grave disappointments happen. I have felt almost incapable of knowing there are things I cannot fix. I strive and I fight and I struggle and I work hard and wear myself out trying to fix and understand. And when I fail over and over again, I get up and fight some more. Then, I hit my limits, the ones I tend not to accept, which makes me sullen, grumpy, withdrawn, and tired.

And yet, I keep fighting. I keep trying to understand. I keep trying to fix. Perhaps you can relate. I think we all have a propensity to act in just this way when financial downturns come, cancer diagnoses occur, people act to harm us, relatives cause drama, disappointment comes our way, car accidents happen, or deep frustrations implant themselves in our minds; when we encounter suffering. We also engage in the same fixing behavior, the same quest for deeper understanding, whenever we gain new reasons for our insecurities or we struggle against poor reputations in town or we fear what others think of us or we worry about how we look.

These are real problems, things we struggle with, and in the face of them, what are we to do? The answer we might first think of, the very first thing that comes to mind, is to be more disciplined in our relationship with God. That will make us feel better. That will solve the issues. That will bring us release. The pursuit of righteousness will address the difficult, miserable, things of life when they come.

But vanity, Qoheleth says. This also is vanity.

I certainly ascribe to the need for discipline. I'm nothing if not disciplined, and my life reflects that. Discipline keeps me going. Without my usual morning routine, I struggle. If I'm unable to follow my usual sermon writing schedule, I struggle. If I'm not exercising on a regular basis, I feel it in my body and soul as both yearn for the release of exercising. Discipline makes my world go round. In fact, this current bout of suffering has interrupted many of my routines, adding to my struggle. The loss of routine fosters insecurity, reminding me in subtle and unsubtle ways that I have less control than I want, which sometimes leads me to try to get more control through discipline.

And such is how we're taught we're supposed to be. Discipline makes things better. Not only by providing stability and the comfort of routine in life, but also because it makes us better disciples. After all, the word disciple is within the word discipline. To really follow Christ, to grow in righteousness, as we're called to do, is to be disciplined.

We all want to be more disciplined, more righteous. That's part of why we go to church. It's why we're disciplined. It's why we have expectations of ourselves and why we hold ourselves to those expectations of discipline and growing in righteousness. And we believe that growing in righteousness will help us understand, will impart wisdom, and perhaps will make life a little easier. There's definitely truth to all of that.

But Qoheleth argues in a way contrary to that thinking. Qoheleth says instead that the righteous get treated like the wicked and the wicked like the righteous. This is just the way of things in the world. He sounds like your grumpy old uncle who, after you describe your problems, says, "Life's a jerk," and then says nothing more.

Life where the unrighteous prosper and the righteous suffer is, according to Qoheleth, inscrutable, inexplicable, beyond our comprehension. It's just the way of life, he says at the end of this scripture. No matter how hard we study God's ways, and no matter how wise some become in the ways of God, none of us will ever have full understanding; we will not, in his words, "find it out." God's ways are beyond our ways, God's rationale for why the righteous are treated as the wicked and vice versa are beyond our comprehension, and so we are simply resigned to this fact: that life is just this way.

To which Qoheleth says vanity. This also is vanity.

This ought to strike us as odd because we tend to think of ourselves as highly capable people. Certainly I think of myself that way. We're taught that we can do anything we put our minds to. We're taught that if we study hard enough, we can understand anything. From a young age, we're taught that we can be anything we want to be, that if we work hard enough, we can get into whatever college we want. We're taught that the world is our oyster, and if we will just apply ourselves hard enough, everything is possible for us.

But Qoheleth says it's in vanity we think that way because we refuse, at a certain level, to accept our limits. That's what Qoheleth has to say to us: We have limits. We cannot comprehend why a good God allows the righteous to be treated as the wicked and vice versa. No matter how wise we may become, we cannot understand the ways of God. They are ultimately inscrutable, unknowable, out of our reach.

And so, it's in vanity we seek to change our circumstances, whatever they may be. Vanity, this is also vanity, Qoheleth would say to us as we try to fix our suffering. Suffering itself is a limit and, fair to say, it reveals just how limited we are.

We like to think of ourselves as limitless, and much of our culture reinforces such a notion. Daily, I use a particular app that subtly conveys such a message. My health care rewards me with up to forty dollars per quarter if I go into this app, check off some habits, and read two short coaching tips that are supposedly about being healthier. Most days, at least one of them focuses on being more productive, talking about how proper rest, diet, exercise, and the like can make us more productive. This is a subtle lie: that we not only can always be more productive, but that we exist primarily or even exclusively to produce! We should not live a healthy lifestyle to be more productive. Yet we find this pervasive lie all across our society.

When we suffer, our production naturally dips. The energies we naturally focused into our labors get redirected to our suffering as we wrestle, deal with hard emotions, and try to accept the expectations we examined in Part 1. Such loss of productivity can leave us feeling helpless, listless, even guilty. But we do not exist to produce, and it's in vanity that we seek to be more productive anyway, because it's a primary way we seek to be limitless in this life.

It's in vanity because all of these things we ultimately cannot fix. We cannot change people; only God can do that. We cannot change relationships on our own; only God can do that. We cannot create justice; only God can do that. We cannot control how other people perceive us; only God can do that. We cannot fix our shortcomings alone; only God can do that. We cannot fix our suffering; only God can do that.

We have limits. There are things in this life that we cannot fix, things over which we have no power. Those are the arenas of faith—the spaces where only God has power. When we push back against our limits, when we try to understand the things we can't and try to fix the things we have no power to fix, we play God. That's why it's vanity: It's us trying to do what only God can do. This doesn't mean we don't try and we don't seek wisdom. No, in order to know where our limits are, we must first try to fix the problems in life, try to understand and comprehend the way of things. We must seek after God through discipline to grow in righteousness, for doing so teaches us where we have limits; where to stop our vain striving and let God be God.

The reality is this: We can either fight against our God-given limits, trying hard to fix or understand what is beyond our ability, or we can let God be God. When we have done everything we can do, when we have sought all the wisdom there is to know and it has yet failed us, when we have tried every fix imaginable and it's not worked, it's time to let go, it's time for release, it's time to declare that life is just that way and we will perhaps never, in the words of Qoheleth, "Find it out." Life sometimes comes with things we cannot control, we cannot understand, we cannot fix; things we cannot work our way out of.

Our discipline and righteousness eventually reach their limits. Spiritual maturity, the kind that grows under discipline and life shared with God, should lead us to know where those limits are and be accepting of them, believing that God will take care of what we cannot.

The point of this scripture is that continuing to try to push past our limits is vanity. It's our attempt to play God. Instead, scripture says to us: Know and accept your limits.

What are we, mere humans, mortal ones as Qoheleth says in Ecclesiastes, to do?

This can sound like reason for resignation, to be resigned to our fate, to sit and be sullen. But there's great power and joy in releasing ourselves from believing that we have the power to fix what we cannot, that we have the power to control what we cannot, and that we have the power to comprehend what we cannot. There's great power in accepting our limitations as humans and great power in allowing God to be God. Just as we saw in Part 1 and especially chapter 8, there's great power in accepting our suffering, the limits we have to resolve hardship, change, insecurity, and fear.

For when we choose to accept that we have limits, when we say, "OK, God, I've done all I can do," we discover the wisdom of Qoheleth in the middle of our scripture: "So I commend enjoyment, for there is nothing better for people under the sun than to eat and drink and enjoy themselves, for this will go with them in their toil through the days of life God gives them under the sun."

Instead of fighting so hard to fix what we cannot, instead of striving so hard to understand what we never will, when we have naturally reached our limits, God says through Qoheleth that it's time to go be happy. It's time to eat, drink, and be merry. It's time to engage in the things God has given us that bring us joy.

This, in fact, is one of the points of a regular sabbath practice. Regular time for rest, set aside and unencumbered by work and obligation, releases us to enjoy the things God has made us to enjoy: gardening, video games, fishing, hiking, woodworking, crafting, watching TV, cooking, and the like.

Qoheleth's call, and indeed God's call on us, is to eat, drink, and be merry, as older translations of this text say. When we try to do what only God can do, we bring much despair into our lives. When we try to fix what only God can fix, we bring much exhaustion into our lives. When we try to control what only God can control, we bring much frustration into our lives. When we try to solve our suffering on our own, we risk getting lost in the land of suffering, becoming increasingly resentful, bitter, and angry.

When we admit that we cannot, we discover that we can—in the midst of the difficult things in life—find joy.

When bad news comes that we cannot understand, it's time to grab some comfort food and sit with a close friend. When family or friends cause drama, it's time to go engage with our favorite hobby. When life is just crappy, it's time to go fish. When people are mean, it's time to go play golf. When someone makes you angry, it's time to go bike riding. And when life gives you great disappointments, it's time to go seek comfort from the presence of loved ones.

Eat, drink, and be merry isn't a call to drown sorrows in food, drink, or partying. It's a reminder that we're made for joy. In joy, God made us, including giving us certain things we naturally enjoy. This means no matter the difficulties of life, joy is offered to us. There are things we naturally enjoy doing, activities that give us great joy and peace and restore our souls. The call, on a regular basis but especially when we have reached our limits, is to go and engage with those.

God offers a different path for me, and for any of us who sound like me. Instead of fighting, striving, struggling, and wearing ourselves into exhaustion to understand what we never will, or to fix what we cannot, or to control the uncontrollable, we're called to go and delight in the things that bring us joy. We're called to let God be

God, both in accepting our limitations and in believing God desires for us to live a life full of joy.

To phrase it another way, we shouldn't let life rob us of joy. Instead, God's call is to go eat, drink, and be merry.

During this time of suffering, I have often preached this message to myself, reminding myself when I start to sulk or retreat or try to control the uncontrollable. In writing, I have found joy. I have also done more reading, much more reading, of a variety of books. I like historical fiction and have found joy in several novels. I have also been doing more walking, not out of exercise discipline but out of the joy of movement, born of being stuck in bed for five weeks, and out of the joy of communing with God in nature.

When we run into limits, it's time to go find some joy. In the past when I reached limits, mindful of the wisdom of Ecclesiastes, I would play the piano. I'm teaching myself to play. I've always wanted to play and I'm musically inclined, having played trombone through college and been a music major my first three semesters of college. Playing piano is one of the things I do when I've hit my limits. It's a way of joy. It's not escapism; the problems still exist. But it's a way of experiencing the joy God designed me for, a way of accepting my limitations. Playing piano is one way I follow Qoheleth's advice to eat, drink, and be merry.

This means that when playing the piano begins to feel like a chore, I stop. When it starts to feel like something I'm trying to achieve, I stop. When it moves from anything other than joy, I stop and return on another day. Consequently, I'm not very good, but that's not the point. The point is joy.

So when you reach your limits, when you face inscrutable problems, when you cannot fix what you want to fix, when you cannot change what you want to change, what do you go do? Better put, in the words of Qoheleth, how do you make merry? What brings you joy?

God's invitation is to accept our limits and then go and eat, drink, and be merry.

This is not escapism. It's embracing the joy, the freedom, that comes from accepting our limits. We are only human; we are not God. We can only do so much. When we learn to accept that, we find the joy of life that allows us to really, truly be happy.

So I commend the wisdom of Qoheleth: Accept your limits and find joy in this life. Let God be God. Part of being disciplined and growing in righteousness is accepting our limitations and choosing to engage with the joys of our lives. It's accepting we are not God, and we do not have control over everything, nor do we have the ability to understand all things. At some point, we all reach our limit, and the disciplined, righteous thing to do is to go find some joy.

No matter the hardships you encounter nor the limitations you face, eat, drink, and be merry, for "this will go well with [you] in [your] toil through the days of life that God gives [you] under the sun" (Ecclesiastes 8:15).

Field Notes

What can you do to eat, drink, and be merry during this time of suffering?

Chapter 15

Look to the Past and Give Thanks

O give thanks to the Lord, for he is good,
  for his steadfast love endures forever.
O give thanks to the God of gods,
  for his steadfast love endures forever.
O give thanks to the Lord of lords,
  for his steadfast love endures forever;
    who alone does great wonders,
  for his steadfast love endures forever;
who by understanding made the heavens,
  for his steadfast love endures forever;
who spread out the earth on the waters,
  for his steadfast love endures forever;
    who made the great lights,
  for his steadfast love endures forever;
    the sun to rule over the day,
  for his steadfast love endures forever;
the moon and stars to rule over the night,
  for his steadfast love endures forever;
who struck Egypt through their firstborn,
  for his steadfast love endures forever;
and brought Israel out from among them,
  for his steadfast love endures forever;
with a strong hand and an outstretched arm,
  for his steadfast love endures forever;

> *who divided the Red Sea in two,*
> *for his steadfast love endures forever;*
> *and made Israel pass through the midst of it,*
> *for his steadfast love endures forever;*
> *but overthrew Pharaoh and his army in the Red Sea,*
> *for his steadfast love endures forever;*
> *who led his people through the wilderness,*
> *for his steadfast love endures forever;*
> *who made water flow from the rock,*
> *for his steadfast love endures forever;*
> *who struck down great kings,*
> *for his steadfast love endures forever;*
> *and killed famous kings,*
> *for his steadfast love endures forever;*
> *Sihon, king of the Amorites,*
> *for his steadfast love endures forever;*
> *and Og, king of Bashan,*
> *for his steadfast love endures forever;*
> *and gave their land as a heritage,*
> *for his steadfast love endures forever;*
> *a heritage to his servant Israel,*
> *for his steadfast love endures forever.*
> *It is he who remembered us in our low estate,*
> *for his steadfast love endures forever;*
> *and rescued us from our foes,*
> *for his steadfast love endures forever;*
> *who gives food to all flesh,*
> *for his steadfast love endures forever.*
> *O give thanks to the God of heaven,*
> *for his steadfast love endures forever.*
> —Psalm 136

WHY DO YOU LOVE Thanksgiving so much?

I get that question every November because I really do love Thanksgiving. I love gathering with friends for a "Friendsgiving" early in the week. On the day itself, I relish the opportunity to slow down, play games and enjoy company, to simply be present with cherished loved ones. On top of that, the weather cools, the leaves are falling, and often the sun is shining. I love Thanksgiving.

I'm even kind of thankful that Thanksgiving is increasingly overshadowed by Christmas. It seems the Christmas season starts somewhere around October 20. So by that measure, by the time we celebrate Thanksgiving, we're about halfway through the Christmas season. But this overshadowing means that Thanksgiving retains a sort of purity, less corrupted by forces of commercialism.

I have many fond, warm memories of Thanksgivings gone by. Perhaps you do, too. Bring to mind those memories, of gathering together, of family and dear friends. Every Thanksgiving, I find reason to say with this psalm, "Give thanks to the Lord for he is good, [God's] steadfast love endures forever" (Psalm 136:1). In fact, I find reason to say it at least twenty-seven times, just as it occurs in the psalm. And I imagine that holds true for all of us reading this chapter; we all have reason to give thanks to God.

Such was also true for the author who penned these words, "The year that is drawing towards its close, has been filled with the blessings of fruitful fields and healthful skies."[27] Those are Abraham Lincoln's words, writing his Thanksgiving Proclamation in 1863. He continues by thanking God for the manifold blessings the country is experiencing. Beautiful words, but let us consider what had happened in the months leading up to this 1863 proclamation.

The Battle of Gettysburg was fresh in the minds of the people. The union had won the battle but at a tremendous cost. A reorganization of the Union armies hadn't produced the results hoped for, and the people had little hope of anything except a continued long, costly, brutal war. In 1863, the people knew death, destruction, and desolation at their doorstep. And in that year, Lincoln continued his suspension of the constitutional right of habeas corpus and issued a draft, the first in the history of the country, causing riots across the north.

Henry Wadsworth Longfellow, American poet of fame, also writing that same year, reflected on the reality of death, destruction, and desolation when he penned these words, "Then from each black accursed mouth, the cannon thundered in the South, and with their sound the carols drowned of peace on earth, good-will to men!"[28] He could speak from personal experience. His son, Charles Appleton Longfellow, had joined the union army against his father's express wishes. In November 1863, he was severely wounded. And so Longfellow continues, "And in despair, I bowed my head. There is no peace on earth, I said: for hate is strong, and mocks the song of peace on earth, good-will to men."[29]

This was the reality for the country in 1863. And yet, Lincoln writes that the year "has been filled with the blessings of fruitful fields and healthful skies." How can he say that, knowing the destruction and devastation? The loss of constitutional rights and the rioting across the north? The death that touched nearly every family across the United States?

There are parallels to our own time. We have come through the pandemic, but we are still living with the global upheaval it caused. We have witnessed wars across the globe, enough devastation and destruction on their own, and then worried that some of these conflicts might lead to regional or even global conflicts.

Then, we must consider the rise in hate. When we talk about being increasingly divided as a nation, too often we're talking about the increase in hate among different groups. How do we give thanks, how do we proclaim that God's steadfast love endures forever, with hate on the rise? With wars around the world? With the threats and challenges we currently know?

Proclaiming, "Give thanks to the Lord for he is good, God's steadfast love endures forever," can feel challenging when, in Longfellow's words, it seems that "hate is strong and mocks the song of peace on earth, goodwill to men."

Perhaps Longfellow understood the times better than Lincoln. Was Lincoln delusional with his words? The rest of Lincoln's 1863 Thanksgiving Proclamation makes some mention of the war but generally gives thanks to God for all the country is, in his word, "enjoying." How could Lincoln write such a thing? What is there to enjoy during a period of destruction, desolation, and hate? Could we, ourselves, utter such words today, mindful of the trouble we know?

I have had troubling Thanksgivings of my own. During one particularly tough Thanksgiving a several years ago, I felt beset from every side and saw no way forward through the sheer conflict and trouble I knew at the time. I knew tremendous suffering. My Thanksgiving that year was full of fear and worry as I gazed upon the desolation and destruction I knew in my life. Perhaps you've known Thanksgivings like that. Maybe you've entered into a Thanksgiving with lots of fear and worry because of what's happening outside of your family. Maybe it's the gathering together with family that led to a hard and fraught Thanksgiving. How do we give thanks when Thanksgivings go wrong, or when life gives us little to no reason to give thanks?

How do we give thanks when journeying through the land of suffering? Such seems counterintuitive. Sure, we can practice Examen, as we saw in chapter 13, seeking to understand where God is moving, but can we really and truly be thankful when suffering so greatly? The United States suffered greatly that year of 1863. Was Lincoln delusional? Maybe he was just focusing on joy, as we discussed in chapter 14? But that feels like a dereliction of duty in some way, or even something worse. Perhaps Wadsworth knew better when he said, "Hate is strong and mocks the song of peace on earth, goodwill to men."

How can we give thanks when suffering?

I brought that question with me to church during that season of life. And there, we sang these words: "Ponder anew what the Almighty can do."[30]

And those words said to me, in the midst of my trouble, "God's not done with you yet, Ted. Give thanks to the Lord, for he is good; his steadfast love endures forever" (Psalm 136:1). And I knew, at that moment, a reassurance only God can provide. While suffering, I knew God would see me through.

I knew this truth not only through this transcendent moment, but because my thoughts went back to my past, to times where I could see how God's steadfast love had endured. I could remember former times of trouble, times when I had worried and feared, and could see how God had brought me through. My past showed me my future: God's steadfast love had endured for me, and so I could "ponder anew what the Almighty could do" for my current suffering.

It seems the best way to know that God's steadfast love endures forever is to see how God's steadfast love has endured forever in our pasts. It's to look back and see how God brought us through times of trouble to the other side. When we do so, we gain the imagination to "ponder anew what the Almighty can do," for we can see how God has brought us through times of conflict and division, times of desolation and destruction, times of hopelessness and despair.

Psalm 136 records just that. Consider verses 10 through 22. They recount Israel's history, the way they have seen God deliver and provide for them. They recount times of war, times of hardship, times of slavery, times of despair, want, and fear. They do not hold back in recounting the challenging parts of their history. But with each recounting, they echo that repeated refrain, "For [God's] steadfast love endures forever." They can look back on their past and see how God has provided, how God has delivered, how God has been present through their suffering. And in looking back, they can see how God's steadfast love brought them through. That's what powers their ability to believe that God will always provide; they can "ponder anew what the Almighty can do" in their future by seeing how God has always provided for them in their past.

That was reason for Thanksgiving.

For us today, it can be reason for thanksgiving, too.

At a meeting of United Methodist churches in South Georgia, I was asked to help lead prayer moments. During a season when we were still reeling from the loss of friends and churches we'd known for years through the current schism in Methodism, I turned to this psalm to help us move forward. I substituted the history of our conference in verses 10 through 22. Together, we gave God thanks for the way God has been with us throughout the history of our annual conference, a history that includes times of "fruitful fields and healthful skies" and times of hardship, including this particular moment. But together, both in joys and sorrows, we proclaimed that God's steadfast love endures forever, so we could "ponder anew what the Almighty could do" during this season of loss.

When we suffer—when we see only destruction and desolation ahead, when it seems that "hate is strong and mocks the song of peace on earth, goodwill to men"—it's time to look back to the past. There, in our own history, the one we can recount just like the psalmist of old, we see how God has moved, how God has provided, and how God has restored. We can see that God's steadfast love does, indeed, endure forever, and so we can give thanks. Not only that, but we can also look to the future with hope, knowing if God has done it before, God can do it again.

Think back on your life. When has God redeemed you from trouble? When has God provided? Where can you see how God's steadfast love has endured forever for you?

Whatever you see, give thanks to God. Let us consider how God's steadfast love has brought us through whatever trials and tribulations we may have known in recent years—the desolation, destruction, fear, and death we may have witnessed and experienced ourselves. Consider that alongside the joys and highs of life, the blessings we have also experienced over the course of the year. How has God redeemed you, brought you to the other side, provided for you, where you can then exclaim, "Give thanks to the Lord, for he is good, for his steadfast love endures forever"?

This is the point of the worksheet provided in Appendix 2. This worksheet incorporates the opening and closing of this psalm, and leaves blanks for the middle, spaces for you to recount God's presence in your history. Where have you known God's deliverance and steadfast love? What challenges and hardships have you known? How have you seen God provide? When you hear the words, "God's steadfast love endures forever," what comes to mind? This is perhaps an extended meditation on the form of Examen discussed in chapter 13.

If the suffering you know makes these questions difficult to answer, hear the words again from that hymn, "Ponder anew what the Almighty can do." God has moved in power, providing for you and your family even through the tough times, though it may take some thinking, some conversation, some pondering, to see what God has done and is doing for you and your family. But God has been faithful in your past, just as God was for the Israelites.

Record what you find there on that worksheet. This can be a great way of praying together, of stimulating conversation as a family, of drawing together in community. As you gather, say how God's steadfast love has endured through your family and friendships forever. Together, just as the Israelites who first wrote this Psalm, you are recounting your history and showing how God's steadfast love has endured forever for you and your kin. We do this annually at Thanksgiving, with whomever gathers at our table. The results stay on that worksheet from Appendix 2 on our refrigerator, a reminder of how God has seen us through and will continue to see us through.

That's been my history. This is why I love Thanksgiving so much. It's an annual chance to reflect, to see where God has moved through the good and especially the bad, so that I may say afresh and anew: God's steadfast love endures forever. It's an opportunity to ponder what the Almighty can do so that no matter what happens between now and next Thanksgiving, we can be assured and rest our faith in that oft-repeated phrase: God's steadfast love endures forever.

It seems Lincoln knew that reality, that God's steadfast love redeems our troubles. He believed God would provide, God would take care, and so it was good and right and true to give God thanks in the midst of devastation, destruction, fear, and death of 1863 because he knew God wasn't done with him yet. God wasn't done with the United States of America yet. So he could give thanks to God despite the troubles that enmeshed, enveloped, enjoined, and enraptured. He could say, "Give thanks to the Lord, for he is good; God's steadfast love endures forever."

And even with his son severely wounded, knowing the devastation and destruction of the Civil War, Longfellow pondered anew what the Almighty can do. After saying in his famous poem, "And in despair I bowed my head; 'There is no peace on earth,' I said; For hate is strong and mocks the song of peace on earth, good-will to men," the very next stanza says this:

"Then pealed the bells more loud and deep: God is not dead; nor doth he sleep! The Wrong shall fail, The Right prevail, with peace on earth, good-will to men."[31]

Longfellow knew: We are God's people, the sheep of his pasture. God will prevail. The wrong shall fail. The trouble we know now will not last forever. God will provide. God will redeem, just as God has done over and over again in our past.

And we, on the other side, will say with Psalm 136, "O give thanks to the Lord, for he is good, for his steadfast love endures forever."

To find hope for the future, look to the past.

Field Notes

Where in your past can you see how God's steadfast love has endured forever, delivering you from trouble? Can you then "ponder anew what the Almighty can do" in your current suffering?

CHAPTER 16

Practice Forgiveness

"Paul, a prisoner of Christ Jesus, and Timothy our brother, To our beloved coworker Philemon, to our sister Apphia, to our fellow soldier Archippus, and to the church in your house: Grace to you and peace from God our Father and the Lord Jesus Christ. I thank my God always when I mention you in my prayers, because I hear of your love for all the saints and your faith toward the Lord Jesus. I pray that the partnership of your faith may become effective as you comprehend all the good that we share in Christ. I have indeed received much joy and encouragement from your love, because the hearts of the saints have been refreshed through you, my brother. For this reason, though I am more than bold enough in Christ to command you to do the right thing, yet I would rather appeal to you on the basis of love—and I, Paul, do this as an old man and now also as a prisoner of Christ Jesus. I am appealing to you for my child, Onesimus, whose father I have become during my imprisonment. Formerly he was useless to you, but now he is indeed useful to you and to me. I am sending him, that is, my own heart, back to you. I wanted to keep him with me so that he might minister to me in your place during my imprisonment for the gospel, but I preferred to do nothing without your consent in order that your good deed might be voluntary and not something forced. Perhaps this is the reason he was separated from you for a while, so that you might have him back for the long term, no longer as a slave but more than a slave, a beloved brother—especially to me but how much more to you, both in the flesh and in the Lord. So if you consider me your partner, welcome him as you would welcome me. If he has wronged you in any way or owes you anything, charge that to me. I, Paul, am writing this with my own hand: I will repay

it. I say nothing about your owing me even your own self. Yes, brother, let me have this benefit from you in the Lord! Refresh my heart in Christ. Confident of your obedience, I am writing to you, knowing that you will do even more than I ask."—Philemon 1-21

FORGIVE US OUR TRESPASSES, as we forgive those who trespass against us.

Churches say it every Sunday. Some of us say it multiple days a week as a part of our prayer practice. My current prayer book has me praying it daily. Right there, in the middle of the Lord's Prayer, the only prayer that Jesus taught us to pray, and the prayer of the church ever since, we pray that line: Forgive us our trespasses, as we forgive those who trespass against us. In my Presbyterian upbringing, I grew up saying it this way: Forgive us our debts, as we forgive our debtors. More contemporary versions of the Lord's Prayer say it this way: Forgive us our sins, as we forgive the sins of others.

No matter how it's translated, the request is clear: God, forgive us our wrongdoings just as we forgive others their wrongdoings.

This means the two are linked in some way.

Does this mean that, in order for God to forgive us, we have to forgive others? Does this mean that God must forgive us first in order for us to be able to forgive others? Or is the relationship symbiotic, with our forgiveness of others feeding God forgiving us, which allows us to forgive others, and round and round we go?

To put all those questions more simply: What does it mean to forgive others?

Philemon provides a guide to answer that question. This book, one of the shortest in scripture, is all about debts, debtors, and forgiveness.

Paul wrote this personal letter while in prison. Where he was exactly is a matter of dispute, but he's definitely in prison, writing a letter to Philemon. The letter is also addressed to the church that meets in his house, suggesting that Philemon is either hosting a house church or is the pastor of that church. And while Paul includes other leaders of that church in the opening of his letter, what he has to say to Philemon is of a very personal nature.

Onesimus is a runaway slave. At least, that's almost certainly what's happened here. Philemon is Onesimus's master and, for whatever reason, Onesimus has run away, probably fleeing with some money or something else of value. Somehow, Onesimus has run into Paul, such that Paul writes to Philemon asking that Onesimus be received back by Philemon graciously, without any outstanding debt. He asks Philemon to forgive Onesimus both his trespasses and his debts, literally.

For Onesimus has an outstanding debt. According to Roman law, for every day he's gone from his master's home, he owes a debt equal to a day's wage. This collects in perpetuity, such that Onesimus owes a large debt. Even though Roman law allowed for slaves to own property and valuables, such that some slaves in the ancient world became wealthier than their masters, it was unlikely that a slave could repay the debt incurred by running away. Onesimus, if he returned or was captured and forced to return, would owe a debt he could never repay.

Paul thinks Philemon should simply forgive that debt. His rationale is clear: God forgave you out of God's love for you, and Onesimus is your brother in Christ, so forgive Onesimus as God has forgiven you. In other words, live out the words of the Lord's Prayer: Forgive us our trespasses, as we forgive those who trespass against us.

Why would Philemon choose to forgive Onesimus, and especially why would he erase the debt owed to him by Onesimus?

We know about debt. Our circumstances are vastly different, for we live in a world where legalized slavery is largely abolished, a world in which we find slavery morally repugnant. As I have considered Philemon and its background in Roman slavery, I have had to look past my own abhorrence to consider Paul's powerful message about forgiveness. For while I cannot relate to slavery, I can relate to debt.

Consider that we have debts we have taken on. We have banks to whom we owe money, perhaps, or other entities. If we're like the average American family, we have tens of thousands of dollars of consumer debt on things like cars and credit cards. Maybe we borrowed from family members or lived off the support of members of our families.

Then, perhaps, we have friends and family who have cost us. Maybe that's because they encouraged us to make a bad investment. Maybe that's because of an inheritance dispute. Maybe that's because we were cheated out of it. Maybe that's because we have relatives who are in and out of rehabs, prisons, and the like and are constantly in need of funds. Whatever the case, we have real people in our lives who owe us a debt of funds, perhaps one that can never be repaid.

So we have people who owe us money, and we owe money ourselves.

Then there are less tangible debts. We have people who owe us a debt of gratitude and have yet to show it. We've worked hard for them, we've gone the extra mile, and we've labored long and hard, yet we receive no thank yous, no appreciation, no show of gratitude at all. I have felt this very real debt at times when someone else was given credit for my hard work. We are left feeling they are indebted to us: a debt of gratitude.

Or we feel that debt of gratitude in a different way. We receive a gift out of the blue, something very thoughtful and meaningful, and we feel we must repay that kindness—a different kind of debt of gratitude.

And then there are times where we are gravely wounded by someone else. They owe us an apology. For their harsh words, for their unkind actions, they need to apologize. We are owed that apology—a debt of remorse and repentance.

Of course, there's the flip side of that as well. We realize that we have done wrong and have yet to apologize for it. We should, but we just can't bring ourselves to do so. And so we have ourselves a debt of remorse and repentance that's owed to someone else.

In these ways, and I'm sure in others, we have debts we carry with us—debts of money, debts of gratitude, and debts of remorse and repentance. Real debts. Real things we either owe to others or things owed to us by others.

And these debts weigh a lot! They burden us. Whether they're financial or less tangible, we know the weight of debt. It's a weight many of us can relate to.

When we carry those debts, they gradually destroy our relationships as they gradually destroy us. Some of us may go to bed too many nights daydreaming about getting even or daydreaming about receiving that gratitude or that apology we're owed. We have those feelings of anger, bitterness, or guilt whenever we see that person. And those feelings, those hard emotions of anger, bitterness, and guilt, gradually eat away at our souls like a disease.

Such is the case when we are thrust into drama we did not choose and experience relational disruption, as we saw in chapter 6. Imagine Simon wanting to get back at the Roman soldier who thrust him into the drama of the crucifixion. I have spent too much time dreaming of getting even with people who have hurt me, or somehow forcing an apology. I have felt anger and resentment, harbored bitterness, feeling owed in significant ways. And those feelings, that debt I think I am owed, weighs on my soul.

If the actions of others have thrust you into this journey through the land of suffering, I imagine you can relate with Philemon and Onesimus. While our circumstances are very different, like Philemon, we're owed debts of various kinds: financial, gratitude, or repentance and remorse. And like Onesimus, we owe others debts of various kinds: financial, gratitude, or repentance and remorse.

And to us, like to Philemon, Paul says forgive them all. Release each other from the debts we carry.

But why should we forgive? Why should we do as Paul commands Philemon? These debts are real and we're owed. To release that debt means we will never receive what we justly deserve. How does that make sense? Why should Philemon forgive Onesimus his debt and his trespasses? What does it mean to forgive—to forgive us our trespasses, as we forgive those who have trespassed against us?

Paul commands Philemon to forgive on the basis of love in verse 9. From there, he unfolds his argument as to why Philemon should release Onesimus from his debt. In this letter, love is the motivation and power of forgiveness.

That's because, as Paul says in 1 Corinthians 13:5, from that beautiful chapter on the nature of love, that love "keeps no record of wrongs." If we love others like God loves us, we keep no record of wrongs against them.

The love God gave to us through his son, Jesus Christ, is a love that keeps no record of wrongs. This is astounding because we can think of many wrongs God could list in a record of wrongs kept against us. We have done the wrong thing, said the wrong thing, and embraced the wrong thing. We have been cheaters, liars, and haters. We have wounded others, and we have been greedy.

This is true of us all, and not just in the academic sense. We each have had moments where each of those qualities was true. We would stand indebted to God if a record of wrongs was kept against us.

We would have debts of gratitude, of repentance and remorse, and even financial debts we would owe God: Debts of gratitude for all that God has given us and for our very life, debts of repentance and remorse for how we have mistreated those gifts and for the ways we have sinned, and financial debts since every cent of wealth attached to our name ultimately belongs to God.

We have debts we would owe God.

But through Jesus, we see how God loves us, choosing to keep no record of wrongs. That's because, as Paul says, love keeps no record of wrongs.

God forgives all our sins, all our trespasses, and thus no debt is held over our heads. We owe God nothing. There is no record of wrong kept against us, and there never has been.

Even though we should owe God a debt we could never repay, we owe God nothing. God's grace means that God gives us the free gift of love, no strings attached. God desires relationship with us and will not allow any action taken by us to stand in the way of that. God has already forgiven us out of God's love for us, expressed as that free gift of God we call grace.

In doing so, God has set the example. Paul explains that example in stating why Philemon should forgive Onesimus. We should treat our human relationships as God has treated us.

In other words, we should keep no record of wrongs. Forgiving others, as God has forgiven us, means to keep no record of wrongs against others. It means keeping no debt ledger, whether that be a debt of gratitude, a debt of remorse and repentance, or a financial debt stemming from someone's wrongdoing.

That's radical. But that's what Paul tells Philemon to do: Keep no record of wrongs. Forgive as God has forgiven you. And that's what God tells all of us to do. Forgive us our debts, as we forgive our debtors. Forgive us our trespasses, as we forgive those who trespass against us. In other words, forgive as God has forgiven us, by keeping no record of wrongs.

Not that our forgiveness of others makes God forgive us but, rather, that our forgiveness of others is how we live out how God has already forgiven us, showing love and grace as God has shown us love and grace.

And here's more good news: Keeping no record of wrongs, holding no debts, is freedom.

That burden you're carrying because of what you feel you're owed? It's gone when you choose to forgive someone a debt owed to you. Those feelings of anger and bitterness? They're gone when you choose to forgive a debt owed to you. Those feelings of guilt? They're gone when you go and offer someone your apology. And when you do, you unburden that person who is carrying a burden because of what they feel they owe you.

There's tremendous freedom in forgiveness. To forgive is to release from debt by keeping no record of wrongs.

That's what Paul encourages Philemon to do: Wipe the slate clean, keep no record of wrongs against Onesimus, to allow them both to experience the freedom of release from debt and restored relationship.

That's what Paul is encouraging us to do through this short letter we call Philemon.

Hearing this encouragement from Paul and ultimately from our loving God, let us turn the question to ourselves: What record of wrongs might we be keeping? Who, in our lives, needs to have their debt forgiven? A spouse? A coworker? A family member? Someone at your church? Someone in the community? Who, in your life, needs their record of wrongs erased?

And also consider: What record of wrongs are you keeping against yourself? What wrongs have you committed? Who in your life needs you to go and offer your forgiveness? What guilt do you need to be released from? How do you need to forgive yourself?

As Christians, we believe God's grace is given to us freely, providing what we need to live life as God is calling us to live with no record of wrongs.

In this moment, pray and ask God for the grace you need to be able to release others from a record of wrongs you keep and to release yourself from any record of wrongs you keep against yourself. Forgive, release those records of wrong, and experience tremendous freedom. It will be challenging; releasing records of wrong will not be easy. But God is with us, God is providing for us, because God loves us. There's grace enough to release those records of wrong we keep.

For me, I find writing things out a helpful strategy. At times, I tell God in prayer, through my prayer journal, the record of wrongs I am keeping. In doing so, I am both inviting God into that wound for healing and giving that record to God to destroy. Sometimes, I write that prayer on paper and then burn it, literally destroying the record of wrongs I was keeping. To do so is not only our Christian duty, but it also frees us from the weight we carry. As I practice this, I feel myself gradually freed of that weight.

Forgiveness means to keep no record of wrongs, just as God keeps no record of wrongs against us. We are loved by God and called to love others as God has loved us. So let us forgive as God has forgiven us. Release the record of wrongs you carry.

Field Notes

What record of wrongs do you carry? Put those in a prayer here, now, and if you feel so led, rip this page out and burn it as a tangible sign of releasing that record of wrongs.

Chapter 17

Pray with Emotional Honesty

O God, why do you cast us off forever?
Why does your anger smoke against the sheep of your pasture?
Remember your congregation, which you acquired long ago,
which you redeemed to be the tribe of your heritage.
Remember Mount Zion, where you came to dwell.
Direct your steps to the perpetual ruins;
the enemy has destroyed everything in the sanctuary.
Your foes have roared within your holy place;
they set up their emblems there.
At the upper entrance they hacked
the wooden trellis with axes.
And then, with hatchets and hammers,
they smashed all its carved work.
They set your sanctuary on fire;
they desecrated the dwelling place of your name,
bringing it to the ground.
They said to themselves, "We will utterly subdue them";
they burned all the meeting places of God in the land.
We do not see our emblems;
there is no longer any prophet,
and there is no one among us who knows how long.
How long, O God, is the foe to scoff?
Is the enemy to revile your name forever?
Why do you hold back your hand;

> *why do you keep your hand in your bosom?*
> *Yet God my King is from of old,*
> *working salvation in the earth.*
> *You divided the sea by your might;*
> *you broke the heads of the dragons in the waters.*
> *You crushed the heads of Leviathan;*
> *you gave him as food for the creatures of the wilderness.*
> *You cut openings for springs and torrents;*
> *you dried up ever-flowing streams.*
> *Yours is the day, yours also the night;*
> *you established the luminaries and the sun.*
> *You have fixed all the bounds of the earth;*
> *you made summer and winter.*
> *Remember this, O Lord, how the enemy scoffs,*
> *and an impious people reviles your name.*
> *Do not deliver the soul of your dove to the wild animals;*
> *do not forget the life of your poor forever.*
> *Have regard for your covenant,*
> *for the dark places of the land are full of the haunts of violence.*
> *Do not let the downtrodden be put to shame;*
> *let the poor and needy praise your name.*
> *Rise up, O God, plead your cause;*
> *remember how the impious scoff at you all day long.*
> *Do not forget the clamor of your foes,*
> *the uproar of your adversaries that goes up continually.*
> —Psalm 74

WHEN THE DARKNESS COMES, what do we do?

One answer: Put on your party hat and forget your sorrows. We all have our party hats so we can party and forget the darkness and hardship: Retail therapy, traveling, hobbies and habits, drinking, overeating favorite foods, going out, dining out. For me, if I'm really feeling sorry for myself, I want a particular greasy fast-food burger. If not for the near constant nausea I've known for the last several months, I would have eaten several at this point! I've learned that about myself. I tend to avoid fast food, but if I'm really in the dumps, that's what I crave. Somehow, that greasy burger makes me forget about my woes for a bit. Whatever your party hat, we all have our rituals of forgetfulness so we can escape the darkness when it comes.

For the darkness comes, sometimes without warning. And so we don our party hats, take ourselves shopping or partying or dining, and forget for a while.

When the darkness comes, what do we do? We forget.

Or at least we do our best to forget, but we all have experienced the kind of darkness that just won't let go, that we just can't forget no matter how hard we try. Suffering is like that; it ushers in a darkness. And when we find ourselves there, we often cry out to God, asking for help. The trouble is that, too often, silence meets our cries, and we wonder if God is even listening. How should we pray and seek God while consumed by the darkness of suffering?

When the darkness comes, what do we do?

While we might try to forget, the people of God praying this psalm just couldn't forget.

You may remember from Sunday school that Jerusalem and the temple were destroyed by the Babylonians. The elite of society were then taken captive to live in Babylon. In this psalm, the authors record their experience of that destruction. They remember how the city was destroyed, how the temple was sacked with sacrilege, how they took axes to the doorframes and hammers to the carvings. The images are branded on their memory. They can't forget the darkness. It was incredibly disorienting.

No amount of retail therapy on Fifth Avenue in Babylon would undo the destruction they'd experienced. No amount of partying on the beaches of ancient Persia could cause them to forget the trauma they'd endured. No Chaldean fast food—no matter how good the food might be—could let them escape what they'd experienced. The disaster, destruction, chaos, has left them disoriented.

They knew the kind of darkness that won't let go.

There have been a few times in my life I knew a darkness that just wouldn't let go. Eight years ago, I found myself in such a darkness. As a family, we'd moved from Macon to Cartersville, Georgia, so I could take what I thought was a dream job: to be a chaplain at a college. The first six weeks were great. But then, in September, there were warning signs. In October, there were threats against my job. In November, there was an attempt to fire me by the college president. That didn't work out, so the president determined to make my life as miserable as possible, hoping I would quit. Daily I went to Human Resources to hear how terrible I was at my job, how it would be best for everyone if I just quit, how much harm I was doing to others, what a terrible person I was. And nightly, I came home and cried or, having run out of tears and being completely emotionally drained, sat numb, doing not much of anything.

That season was an incredibly difficult, terrible, dark time. I have known the kind of darkness that won't let go. I needed out. I needed relief. I felt like a failure, even though I had done nothing wrong except to run afoul of the president. And I hadn't even meant to run afoul; it just happened.

Then I felt terribly guilty on top of everything else. I'd moved my family up to Cartersville, leaving a life in Macon we loved. We'd sold our house and bought a new house and now looked to have to sell that one, too. I wasn't emotionally available to Dana or my children; I was just constantly emotionally drained. I had nothing left to give but absolutely felt I should. I felt not only that I had somehow failed at my job, and maybe even at my calling to be a pastor, but that I had also failed as a husband and father. I knew a darkness that just wouldn't let go.

Suffering can be like that. I imagine, as you read, you can think of such moments from your own life: When a well-made decision turns out to have been wrong, sometimes the darkness won't let go. When the best laid plans turn to chaos, sometimes the darkness won't let go. When terrible illness suddenly strikes a loved one and threatens their life, sometimes the darkness won't let go. When our finances quickly collapse, sometimes the darkness won't let go. When death strikes quickly and mercilessly, sometimes the darkness won't let go. When a family suddenly ruptures, sometimes the darkness won't let go.

The disaster, destruction, and chaos leave us disoriented.

That was certainly my experience while in Cartersville. I had doubts about whether I had made the right decision to move up there, about whether or not I had failed, but I also had doubts about God. How could God lead me to such a time? Why would God allow it to happen? I thought God had a plan for my life. I thought it was God's will that we move there. I thought God would protect me from harm. I was experiencing none of that. So I shared all those doubts with God in prayer. My prayer journal from that time is angry and full of those kinds of prayers of doubt, just like we find in the Psalms.

It's times like this when it gets tempting to try to forget—to buy the new thing and be excited about it so you can forget the pain, to start a new significant relationship so you can forget the pain of the old, to go on an eating or drinking binge and do whatever feels good, to eat the double quarter pounder with cheese, to make yourself happy, so you can enjoy pleasure and forget the pain.

To forget is tempting. But to forget is only temporary at best. Sometimes our efforts to forget fail completely. Sometimes the darkness is so overwhelming that no pleasure can undo the pain. That was certainly my experience in Cartersville.

When we experience that kind of darkness, what do we do? When a well-made decision turns out to have been wrong and God's plan isn't evident, what do we do? When the best laid plans turn to chaos and God hasn't worked all things together for our good yet, what do we do? When terrible illness suddenly strikes a loved one and threatens their life and God doesn't seem to solve it, what do we do? When our finances quickly collapse and God doesn't provide immediately, what do we do? When death strikes quickly and mercilessly and God feels absent in our pain, what do we do? When a family suddenly ruptures and there's no restoration, what do we do?

When the darkness comes, what do we do? Let's look to the Psalms. In their candor, they provide us with our answer to that question.

Psalm 74 is a great example. The psalmist conveys the feelings of the gathered community without holding back. The people of God, faced with the destruction of their temple and way of life, held in captivity, pray the darkness they're experiencing right back to God.

In this psalm, the people are sitting in the darkness of exile in Babylon. You may recall that they landed there because of the people's sinfulness. They became intoxicated with their wealth and power, and it made them blind to the danger they faced. They forgot their loyalty to God and turned to worship other gods, too. With their attention diverted away from God, they suffered the natural consequences of their actions.

But by the time we get to this psalm, the people have been suffering for a long time. They have long ago repented. In fact, they've repented over and over again. If you've ever apologized to someone and not received forgiveness, this is how they feel. They've apologized to God, they've done all they're supposed to do to make amends, but God feels absent anyway.

And they can no longer stand the silence, so they speak their anger, bitterness, and resentment to God in prayer. They ask God in verses 10 and 11, "How long, O God, is the foe to scoff? Is the enemy to revile your name forever? Why do you hold back your hand; why do you keep your hand in your bosom?" Indeed, the psalm opens with these angry words: "O God, why do you cast us off forever? Why does your anger smoke against the sheep of your pasture?" They tell God he's forgotten them. They tell God what God should be doing. They're clearly very angry and don't shy away from showing that anger to God. They feel abandoned, forgotten.

And so they tell God about it! They don't shy away. They tell God exactly how they feel. They pray the darkness back to God.

Which is the first way the Psalms show us how to handle the darkness: Pray the darkness back to God. Just like in my prayer journal, they tell God all about what they're experiencing and how they're suffering. To pray the darkness back to God is to follow the witness of our forebears in the faith.

And then, they do something else essential: They remember God's character. "Yet God my king is from old, working salvation in the earth. You [God] divided the sea by your might; you broke the heads of the dragons in the waters. You crushed the heads of Leviathan; you gave him as food for the creatures of the wilderness. You cut openings for springs and torrents; you dried up ever-flowing streams. Yours is the day, yours also the night; you established the luminaries and the sun. You have fixed all the bounds of the earth; you made summer and winter," they declare in verses 12 through 17.

They haven't forgotten who God is. God is all powerful, as seen in how God can create from nothing and destroy even the greatest beasts they know, like dragons and sea monsters. If God can do all that, God can do for them. And they still believe that God will.

They know who God is. They are convinced God will provide because God has provided in the past. They look back to their past to find faith and hope for their future. If God has, God will. They know God can be trusted. As angry, as conflicted, as frustrated, as forgotten as they feel, they yet say to God, "Look, this is who you are. This is who we know you to be. And so we believe that you will yet provide. You will come and work on our behalf." They remember who God is and find hope in God's character.

When the darkness comes, what do we do? We pray the darkness back to God, mindful of God's character. When a well-made decision turns out to have been wrong and God's plan isn't evident, we pray the darkness back to God, mindful that God redeems the bad things that happen to us. When the best laid plans turn to chaos and God hasn't worked all things together for our good yet, we pray the darkness back to God, mindful that God makes all things new again. When terrible illness suddenly strikes a loved one and threatens their life and God doesn't seem to solve it, we pray the darkness back to God, mindful that God takes care of us. When our finances quickly collapse and God doesn't provide prosperity, we pray the darkness back to God, mindful that God provides for us. When death strikes quickly and mercilessly and God feels absent, we pray the darkness back to God, mindful that God said to us, "Never will I leave you." When a family suddenly ruptures and there's no restoration, we pray the darkness back to God, mindful that God is the great healer. When the darkness comes, we pray the darkness back to God, remembering in our prayers who God is to find hope for our future.

It may seem or feel wrong to pray in such a way. The Psalms are replete with examples of such prayers, and yet we ourselves may not often pray this way. Sometimes, before I offer such a prayer, I pause in my own prayer journal. We, if we are people of faith, have tremendous respect for God. But we also know that God knows our hearts and sees into our being. God sees if we have doubt, if we are despairing, if we have little faith, if we are angry with God himself! To pray such back to God, offering it verbally, in our heads, or in a prayer journal, is cathartic: It puts the power to address our doubt, despair, faithlessness, and anger in God's hands.

We must pray this way, following the example of the Psalms, for there we find healing.

Whatever darkness you know, God is faithful; the light of God will break into the darkness, for just as we see at creation, just as we see on the cross, just as we see for the people of God in exile who wrote this psalm, the darkness didn't have the final word. Light broke in at creation, light broke through in the resurrection, and the people of God were led back to Jerusalem as God provided restoration. Whatever darkness we might know, the light will always break through.

In Cartersville, God did a great work in my life. Standing at church during Advent, for December was the worst of the darkness for me, we sang a carol I'd never heard before titled, "I Want to Walk as a Child of the Light." In that hymn, the refrain says, "In him [meaning Jesus] there is no darkness at all. The night and the day are both alike. The Lamb is the light of the city of God. Shine in my heart, Lord Jesus."[32]

I lost my composure in church. The words hit me like a ton of bricks: "Stop trying to usher the darkness away on your own, Ted. Jesus Christ is the light. There is no darkness in him. He will take care of you. He will provide. Don't know how. Don't know when. But I know he will."

So pray the darkness back to him, and remember his promises, for the light will one day break through!

I did just that. And eventually, the light shone again. The bishop appointed me to a temporary church so I didn't have to spend the spring at the college where I worked, which was a huge relief. Then I was appointed the following June to Eastman, Georgia, and found healing there. I saw the light of Christ again, and it ushered away my darkness. In fact, I have experienced much redemption, as God has taken my suffering and used it to help others. God has turned my mourning into dancing, my despair into hope, my anger into understanding, and my deep sorrow into joy.

So while we're in the darkness, let us not try to forget, but rather pray the darkness back to God, remembering in our prayers who God is to find hope for our future. Just as I found on that day in Advent during my terrible time of darkness, we have this hope and promise from God: No matter the darkness that consumes, the light will always break through.

Field Notes

Take this space, and this moment, to offer an honest prayer to God about your suffering.

Chapter 18

Go to Nature

Praise the Lord!
Praise the Lord from the heavens;
　praise him in the heights!
Praise him, all his angels;
　praise him, all his host!
Praise him, sun and moon;
　praise him, all you shining stars!
Praise him, you highest heavens
　and you waters above the heavens!
Let them praise the name of the Lord,
for he commanded and they were created.
He established them forever and ever;
he fixed their bounds, which cannot be passed.
Praise the Lord from the earth,
　you sea monsters and all deeps,
fire and hail, snow and frost,
　stormy wind fulfilling his command!
Mountains and all hills,
　fruit trees and all cedars!
Wild animals and all cattle,
　creeping things and flying birds!
Kings of the earth and all peoples,
　princes and all rulers of the earth!
Young men and women alike,

> *old and young together!*
> *Let them praise the name of the Lord,*
> *for his name alone is exalted;*
> *his glory is above earth and heaven.*
> *He has raised up a horn for his people,*
> *praise for all his faithful,*
> *for the people of Israel who are close to him.*
> *Praise the Lord!*
> —Psalm 148

NOT LONG AGO, I took a spiritual pilgrimage. I went to a place that's near and dear to my heart—a place where the grounds, where the buildings, where the trees and the grass, where the sidewalks and roads, all connect my soul with God in a deep and profound way. I went to a place where I felt like I could access God a little more easily, a little more readily. I went to a space that's inspiring, that's uplifting, that feels to me like holy ground.

It wasn't a monastery. It wasn't a church. It wasn't a religious enclave. I went to Emory University.

I went there because for me, there's just something about being outside on Emory's campus. When I attended seminary there, the grounds became special to me. Often, while walking from building to building during seminary, among the shade trees and flowers, I would find myself enraptured, encountering God afresh and anew.

For all of us, we have spaces where we find God. Lately, I encounter God afresh and anew on my walks. These walks are sometimes simply around a loop in my neighborhood. Sometimes I drive to Middle Georgia State University and walk around a lake they have there, calmed by the water and admiring the sky, or the clouds, or the trees beginning to bud. Getting out in nature connects my soul to God in a unique and powerful way. I am sure that you can relate to places and spaces, to hikes and regular commutes, to times of being outside that your soul finds a deeper connect to God.

There are many moments in life when our souls sense that they are in the presence of the praise of God, many times when our depth connects with God's depth because of a place and space. Sometimes, it's a forest or a beach or a mountain. Sometimes it's the bird that flies across our path or watching the seasons change through the trees. Sometimes, it's catching a glimpse of the sun as it finally breaks through the clouds. As I write, the sun shines brightly on my face through the windows of our cabin in Western North Carolina, gradually making its way down below the mountains that shine off in the distance.

Nature can take our breath away through its beauty and majesty, connecting our depth to God's depth. Our souls sense in these moments the depth, the beauty, the wonder of the God who created nature. In these moments, we sense in the deepest part of our being that we are in the presence of the praise of God.

Such is what the psalmist has in mind this morning. All around him, he hears, senses, the praise of God. If the sun could talk, it would sing the praise of the Lord. If the snow could talk, it would sing the praise of the Lord. If the sea monsters could talk, they would sing the praise of the Lord. If creation could talk, it would sing the praise of the Lord.

For indeed, creation returns praise to God. In the sunsets and sunrises, in the wonder and mystery of the universe and the stars, in a walk through a forest on a beautiful day, our souls sense the praise of God because the sun and the stars and the trees are all in constant praise of God.

Just as the highest heavens, the creatures of the earth, the mountains and the trees, all praise the Lord, the maker of heaven and earth. We see God's glory, we are surrounded by God's glory, every time we enter nature, for in creation, we see a reflection of God's magnificence. I believe the author of this psalm would have gotten along quite well with St. Francis of Assisi, the author of a poem immortalized in a famous hymn, "All Creatures of Our God and King."[33]

I wondered to myself one day just how exactly nature conveys God's magnificence. What is it about nature, about creation, that seems to connect our depth with God's depth, our souls with God?

So I left the office early that day to wander. I went for a walk in the arboretum at Wesleyan College, not far from my house. I parked the car by the tennis courts and walked down the path between the courts and the trees to enter the trails. Down the path I walked, glancing around me, my mind racing with all the thoughts of things to do at work, about how much time I had left before I had to get to school to pick up Jackson, of cares and concerns of my personal life.

But as I walked down the path, a funny thing happened. The trees began to stand out in their green glory. I noticed how the brilliant green color made the beautiful blue sky stand out in its own brilliance. I noticed the leaves moving in the wind and suddenly realized a wonderful cooling breeze enveloped me on that path. I looked down to my feet and saw how rich the brown color of the path was, how well worn from good maintenance and lots of use.

My mind slowed down and my ears opened up. I heard birds chirping. A horn suddenly blew and an engine roared, interrupting the moment of tranquility, but it came readily back, wrapping me in nothing other than the peace of God.

In that peace, my deep called to God's deep. My soul connected with God through simply being in the presence of God's creation. Nature has the power to do that, for within nature, we are encircled in one extravagant, elegant, and infinite worship service.

Nature surrounds us with the praise of God. When we walk out of our homes, when we walk through parking lots, when we walk in and out of shops and workplaces, when we roll down the windows of our car and let in the wind, we enter a worship service, for all of nature around us is engaged in the never-ending praise of God. The trees and the grass, the wind and the waves, the ocean and the land, the birds and the crawling creatures, the stars and the sky, do talk. In their very existence, they all sing the praise of the Lord. We live and move and have our being in the midst of an infinite worship service.

What, then, are we to make of natural disasters?

As I write, it is tornado season, a time when severe thunderstorms can bring significant damage. Over the course of the winter, we experienced some flooding in this area—minor to be sure, but yet still causing some damage. During the fall, ironically, we experienced a drought that led to water shortages. All of us know of reports of terrible hurricanes, earthquakes, tsunamis, and other natural disasters wreaking havoc and causing much destruction and desolation.

When the earth quakes, when the storms come, when the rains flood, what are we to make of this created order that returns praise to God? Do the quakes, the storms, and the floods sing the praise of God, too?

Creation can be beautiful and terrifying, sometimes at the same time. The astronaut and now United States Senator Mark Kelly, before returning to earth from the International Space Station, took a photo of Winter Storm Jonas, a huge blizzard that enveloped the mid-Atlantic and northeast one January. It was magnificent to see from space, beautiful, but I thought of how it must have been anything but beautiful to those in the midst of it, below the clouds Kelly could see from space.

From earth orbit, the blizzard certainly seemed to praise God. But from earth's surface, the storm seemed more bad than good. Nature contains within it both order and chaos. The order is inspiring, deep, and beautiful, causing our deep to be connected with God's deep. But in the chaos, we find desperation and horror. Does the chaos return praise to God? How does chaos fit into the infinite worship service happening around us in nature?

The answer is the sea monster.

The psalmist gives us a litany of all the things that should praise God. Most all of what he mentions we know of in our lives today: the heavens, the skies, the angels, the snow and frost, the wind, the creatures of the ground and air, human beings. These things we know of and can relate to how they praise God in their beauty and majesty.

Into this list, in verse 7, he throws in sea monsters.

For ancient Israel—indeed, for neighboring ancient cultures—nothing was more chaotic than the sea. It could turn on sailors without warning, going from tranquil to turbulent. One moment, the fishermen could be catching lots of normal fish; the next, a giant sea monster comes to the surface, threatening the ship. We might understand these monsters as large whales or sharks or even a dolphin, but for the ancient peoples, these were nothing less than Moby Dick.

In fact, the ancient peoples believed the sea monsters controlled the sea. They could make tranquil waters turbulent and turn them back again. That's why so many other ancient societies around Israel worshipped the sea monsters and made offerings to them or to the gods of the sea to control the monsters. Such control would equal order for the seas, giving them peaceful crossings and good catches of fish. Sea monsters represented for ancient Israel the chaos of the seas.

Then, the psalmist continues with a litany of other chaotic things: fire and hail, snow and frost, stormy winds. For a primarily agrarian society, these were not beautiful things, like a fire in a fireplace on a cold winter day when freshly fallen snow covers the ground. No, these were reasons to fear nature, to fear its chaos, for they were primarily an agrarian society and all these agents of chaos wreak havoc on farming.

Indeed, verses 7 and 8 are a call not for the beautiful aspects of nature to praise God, but for the chaotic aspects to praise God as well. Praise God, you sea monsters who kill sailors and withhold catches of fish. Praise God, you snow and frost that kill plant life. Praise God, you earthquakes that kill and destroy civilization. Praise God, you tornadoes that strike fear and hurt into the lives of humanity, your images. Praise God, you chaos.

Praise the Lord!

The psalmist tells us that even the chaos joins in this never-ending worship service of creation that surrounds us. The chaos joins in worship because the psalmist tells us the sea monsters, the snow and frost, the fire and hail, the stormy winds are all at God's command.

God is a God of order, not a God of chaos. Nature reveals to us some of the essential characteristics of who God is and is not: God is beautiful, not monstrous; majestic, not wretched; full of glory, not shame; honorable, not disgraceful; and ordering, not chaotic.

We live now in a creation, though, that demonstrates both characteristics—a creation that is in between beautiful and monstrous, majesty and wretchedness, glory and shame, honor and disgrace, and order and chaos. We live now in a creation that is in between: in between Christ's first and second coming, in between order and chaos. In that in-between time, goodness and mercy and grace rule the day, but evil and its sibling, chaos, still exist and will continue to exist until that second coming. Sometimes, the chaotic parts of nature will rear their head and we'll face sea monsters of our own: earthquakes, tornadoes, floods, damaging stormy winds, and the like.

But it's God's goodness, grace, and mercy that leads God to always bring order out of the chaos. Just as for a time, chaos may win in our lives, and just as for a time, chaos won when Jesus was on the cross, God will always bring order back to the chaos because God is a God of order.

In the seasons that change, in the shoot that comes out of the stump, in the grass that grows despite the weeds, we see God reordering the chaos. In the earth that heals itself after an earthquake, in the farmland that heals despite a tornado's path, in the trees that learn to stand upright again after a mighty wind, we see God reordering the chaos. God is a God of life, not of death, and life always finds a way because God is a God of order, not chaos..

It's God's good pleasure to bring order back to our chaos. And in nature's ability to restore after chaos, in God's ordering out of chaos, we find even more reason in creation to return praise to God. Indeed, the sea monsters of life, the chaos, offer praise to God because they reveal God's power, God's sovereignty, God's strength, through God's order.

All of nature reveals God to us, teaches us about who God is, because it demonstrates through its life, through its order and chaos, that our God does, in fact, reign. It demonstrates that goodness and mercy will indeed follow us all the days of our lives. Creation reveals the beauty, majesty, glory, honor, and order of our infinite God.

At the high-water moments of the life of faith, it's easy to go to nature and discover this infinite God as our depth senses creation returning praise to its creator. And even in seasons of drought spiritually, in times when our own praise feels silenced, times of chaos, our depth still senses creation returning praise. Our deep calls to God's deep, not only in the high-water moments of faith, but also in the dry seasons. Our souls are always seeking connection with their creator, and we find that connection, always, in creation.

Creation not only reveals God's resurrection power for itself, but it can also serve as a vessel for the resurrection of our own souls in the dry seasons of faith. To go into nature in these times of doubting God, of anger toward God, of sadness and despair in life, is to discover the resurrection power that will not only enliven our souls again, but will also restore our own voices to the praise of our beautiful, majestic, gloried, honorable, and ordering God.

So when the sea monsters of life come, when the chaos threatens the stability of your faith, in the suffering you know, go to creation. Enter its infinite worship service. Sometimes in life, our voices of praise are silenced by life's troubles, demands, stresses, and challenges. Go into creation anyway. Enter the worship service around you by walking the trails, staring at the night sky, delighting in the sunlight, until you find your voice again. We can enter the infinite worship service in creation anytime and find our ability to praise resurrected.

Go into nature to discover how wide, how deep, how long is the love of a God who brings order to chaos, who resurrects life out of death. Go to creation to discover the beauty, the majesty, the glory, the honor, and the order of God. Even when I feel terrible, even when I lack in energy, I yet still go for walks, for I need, in the midst of my suffering, to be reminded that God orders the chaos, even the chaos I know in my suffering.

Our deep calls to God's deep. Our souls yearn for God's soul. And we find that connection, no matter the chaos that ensues, no matter the silencing of our praise, when we go into the infinite worship service that surrounds us in creation.

Praise the Lord.

Field Notes

How can you incorporate times in nature into your routine to take your suffering into the infinite worship service?

CHAPTER 19

Focus on what Matters

"You have wearied the Lord with your words. Yet you say, 'How have we wearied him?' By saying, 'All who do evil are good in the sight of the Lord, and he delights in them.' Or by asking, 'Where is the God of justice?' See, I am sending my messenger to prepare the way before me, and the Lord whom you seek will suddenly come to his temple. The messenger of the covenant in whom you delight—indeed, he is coming, says the Lord of hosts. But who can endure the day of his coming, and who can stand when he appears? For he is like a refiner's fire and like washers' soap; he will sit as a refiner and purifier of silver, and he will purify the descendants of Levi and refine them like gold and silver, until they present offerings to the Lord in righteousness. Then the offering of Judah and Jerusalem will be pleasing to the Lord, as in the days of old and as in former years. Then I will draw near to you for judgment; I will be swift to bear witness against the sorcerers, against the adulterers, against those who swear falsely, against those who oppress the hired workers in their wages, the widow, and the orphan, against those who thrust aside the alien and do not fear me, says the Lord of hosts. For I the Lord do not change; therefore you, O children of Jacob, have not perished."—Malachi 2:17-3:6

THE VAPOR ROSE IN THE AIR, speaking to me.

I'd bought a humidifier. At our cabin in Western North Carolina, we only have baseboard heat. With an average temperature this past January in the low twenties, it ran quite a bit, drying out the air. Dry air is hard on recovering sinuses and lungs. So I bought a humidifier.

Sitting on the couch, I watched vapor from the humidifier rise in the air, effervescent and then suddenly gone. My thoughts turned to Ecclesiastes, where the author frequently uses the word *havel* to describe life. In Hebrew, *havel* can mean vapor, a wisp of wind—something that's here for a just a moment and gone. Life is that way; our lives are but a bit of vapor, effervescent and then gone. And that's not bad news. It's a call to attention to say that, in our short lives, what we do and how we spend our infinitesimal allotment of time matters.

My computer's name, in fact, is Havel—a reminder in the midst of all the details and demands of work that what I do with my tiny allotment of time matters, that what will ring in eternity is how I raise my children, the way my life impacts the lives of others, and ultimately, how I seek and live out God's love, allowing that love to make something tremendous out of my life. Which means that, quite often, the work I do on my computer is havel.

As I watched the vapor rise from the humidifier, my thoughts turned these profound considerations. Then, I returned to my book, a book that I thought was about the history of a storied brand of bourbon, but turned out to be so much more. And I thought, as I read this profound book, "I need to make some changes. I've lost focus on what matters."

God had a refining message for me.

Malachi is a Hebrew word that means "messenger." It's an apt title for a prophet. He's come to deliver a message to the people of Israel, a message delivered late in the Old Testament's history. After Malachi and Esther, scripture (at least in Protestant bibles) becomes silent for about four hundred years. That's the time period between the end of the Old Testament's writings and the earliest writing in the New Testament, 1 Thessalonians.

So this is a message that stays with the people for quite a while. This messenger, Malachi, is bringing a message that another messenger is coming. We know that messenger is first John the Baptist and then Jesus, but for the people at the time, they just know that God will come and send them a message.

Why is God sending them a message? Because they've been making accusations against God and God is weary of it.

They've been asking God: "Where is the God of justice?" rhetorically saying that he's not to be found. And then they've been accusing God, saying, "All who do evil are good in the sight of the Lord; and he delights in them." They're making accusations against God, saying that God is not living up to God's promises. They feel there is no justice, that God is rewarding evildoers, and they are very frustrated that God would do so. And in making these accusations, they're praying with emotional honesty, just like we discussed in Chapter 17. They're doing what we should do: telling God exactly how they feel.

But when we choose to pray that way—being emotionally honest with God, keeping it real—we must be mindful that we might not like the message we receive back, a message like this one: Refining is hard.

That's the message Malachi brings. And indeed, it was the message eventually brought by John the Baptist and Jesus. The messenger is coming to deliver God's word that a period of refinement is coming, a period of difficulty, challenge, and hardship. So Malachi rightly asks, "Who can stand his coming?" For who can stand when God comes and refines?

Note the examples Malachi uses: refining soap, which if you've ever seen it done, is tremendously hard work and hard on the soap itself. Or the purification of metals in forges, full of fire and heat that burns away imperfections. These images convey a hard truth about refining: It's not a pleasant experience.

And yet, refining is coming. And so the message remains: Refining is hard.

God will render judgment. That's the word here, against the ways they've been living their lives, against those who are doing the wrong thing, against the people for having lost their way. That's a tough message, but that's what God has to say in response to their accusations, to their emotionally honest prayer lives. God says, "You think I'm the problem. Really, it's your failure to be in right relationship with me. I find you wanting, and so I will refine you." In other words, God renders judgment over them.

None of us want someone to render judgment over us, especially if that someone is God, whose judgment is always correct. But sometimes, rendering judgment brings about a necessary and good period of refinement.

Such was true at the start of my professional career. I arrived at Mercer University, my first full-time job after going to graduate school for student affairs, with a head full of answers, a know-it-all sensibility, and a desire to demonstrate my greatness. I was, to a fault, full of myself. My boss, the one who had hired me with great expectation, was quickly disappointed.

When I had the gall to come in and ask for a raise after only being on the job for five months, she lost it. I later learned this was a rare moment for her; she always kept her composure. But not that day. She let me have it. And in letting me have it, she was really reflecting back to me my egotism, my self-centeredness, my grandiosity, and calling it out. She rendered judgment over me. And that was exactly what I needed.

I was sufficiently humbled and I have not been the same since—in a good way. It started a refining process for me and deepened my self-awareness. Having judgment rendered over me wasn't easy, but it was good.

I was refined.

I imagine many of us have had bosses or parents or mentors in our lives who have humbled us in the past. We have had those who have spoken truth into our lives that was hard to hear, but necessary to hear, bringing a truth that allowed us to grow, to flourish, to become better. A truth that refined.

Refining is hard, indeed, but it is good.

And that's the point Malachi wants us to hear today. It's the point that John the Baptist was making from the wilderness as he "prepared the way for the Lord" and "made straight his paths." It was a point Jesus made often. We can be full of religiosity but, no matter how religious we are, no matter how good we think our relationship with God is, we all stand in need of refining.

We stand in need of having our imperfections worked out. We stand in need of having our rough edges hewn. We all stand in need of growing in our faith through the refining work God is doing in our lives.

In The United Methodist Church, we call that refining process sanctification. It's a way of describing the journey of growing in faith, of falling deeper in love with God. It's a journey of becoming more and more a representative of God's kingdom on this earth, the peaceable kingdom that brings hope and justice to the world. Another way to say that is this: God means to make tremendous things of us; not just for our own benefit but for the benefit of the world as we live out the love of God that grows within us.

Sanctification, this refining, comes through worship and what we do beyond worship to engage with God. Sunday school classes, small groups, personal times of prayer or scripture reading, serving through the church, all of these and more are ways we are sanctified, refined.

Refining also comes through suffering. Times of suffering, when we have come through to the otherwise of the land of suffering, can make us better people, better servants of God, a people who heal others.

God refines us. But we have a choice of whether or not we will participate in that refinement. God will come to us with messages, just like here in Malachi, out of God's love for us and desire to realize the tremendous things God means to make of us.

But we have a choice of whether or not we will participate. We can opt out of participation in being refined, but God will keep coming. The refining God brings will often be like a fire: It will burn and it will be hard, like that day in my boss's office. Judgment will sometimes be rendered. Refining is very hard, indeed.

But refining is good. For when we submit to be refined, we become ever-greater forces for justice and righteousness, for good, in this world. We become the tremendous thing God means to make of us; a powerful witness to the love of God that transforms lives, families, and our world.

Refining is hard, but it is good.

Watching that vapor rise at the cabin while reading that book, I thought to myself, "I need to make some changes. I've lost focus on what matters." God was speaking a refining message to me. I'd been praying with emotional honesty and here, in this moment, came a messenger in a strange form: the mist of a humidifier and a profound book by a sports writer named Wright Thompson, a book called *Pappyland*.[34]

Reading this book I initially thought was about bourbon, the author began to quote one of my favorite contemplative theologians, Thomas Merton. Turns out, *Pappyland* really lived into the second part of its subtitle by talking about "things that last."

Reading Thomas Merton and watching the vapor rise, I found myself thinking about my life, thinking about what I'm doing with my time, considering the stressors I felt both before I got so sick and from being so sick. There's tremendous opportunity in suffering—there's time to reflect, time to ask hard questions and consider the answers, time to evaluate and allow those discoveries to refine.

Merton says, as quoted in this book, "Why, then, do we continue to pursue joys without substance .... Because the pursuit itself has become our only substitute for joy. Unable to rest in anything we achieve, we determine to forget our discontent in a ceaseless quest for new satisfaction. In this pursuit, desire itself becomes our chief satisfaction."[35]

In that moment of reading, those words resonated deeply. I knew I was unable to rest in anything I achieved. Too often, the pursuit itself was my joy; in other words, I stayed busy without questioning whether I needed to be busy because being busy was where I went looking for much of my joy. The desire to build, create, and foster influence and reputation had become my chief satisfaction.

For example, I considered how I thought I had reached a vocational height very early in my career when appointed to Mulberry Street

United Methodist Church, the last church I served. We clergy have a bad habit of ranking churches, and I had reached the top of the ranks and done so at a relatively young age. I figured I would find contentment, no longer striving for greater things. I was wrong. I could not rest in that achievement or any others. Desire itself, the need to stay busy, the need to keep achieving, had replaced true sources of joy.

That was the refining message. I was ceaselessly striving because I was trying to strive for joy in this life, when in fact the striving itself was what kept me from experiencing joy! That's a hard message for a go-getter like me to hear.

Indeed, refining is hard.

Throughout the chapter in *Pappyland* where he quotes Thomas Merton, Wright Thompson frequently uses the word "strive." The striving for things becomes the chief focus of life, sometimes even to the point that we don't know why we're striving anymore. We seek to build things, like careers or reputations or influence, not even sure at some point why we're still building, still striving, still pursuing. At that point, as Merton says, the act of striving, pursuing, working so hard, has become "our only substitute for joy ... our chief satisfaction." We keep moving and stay busy, always doing more, because it's all we know to do and the only way we know to find joy. But in reality, the striving crushes and distracts from true joy in this life. The striving is havel, and like Ecclesiastes says, living such a life of striving is unsatisfying, unhappy, a chasing after the wind.

Thompson goes on to say, in his experience from interviewing and getting to know many sports celebrities through his writing, he has found that success is just another form of currency. He says you can spend success on trying to get more success—trying to become rich, famous, and powerful—or on having the life you've always wanted.

Sitting there, watching the mist rise, thinking about havel, the short span of my life, and about things that last, I realized I already have the life I've always wanted. In fact, I thought back to high school and realized I have a life today far beyond my imaginings then. There's no need to strive for more.

I realized in that moment I needed to stop pursuing, desiring, and striving. I needed to start simply being: being myself, being who God made me to be, and resting in God's image inside of me. Simply be, and let God work through me, was the refining message I got from God.

And it's a message that's proven to be incredibly freeing: free from much of the stress I put on myself, free from a drive for work that was somewhere past overdrive, free from the need to achieve, free from the need to constantly be proving myself.

It also prepared me for future suffering. I got this refining message in January. Three months later, that same church that I thought indicated my success fired me, having grown impatient with my health challenges. Because I had learned to look for value in the "things that last," as Thompson says, and not in my career, I have better weathered this latest storm. My identity feels solid, my sense of relationship with God healthy, because I do not find my selfhood in part or whole in my vocation.

I am a better human because of this process of refining. In fact, even as I see the benefit today, I am still drawing lessons from this refining message.

God had a message for me because God means to make something tremendous of me so that God's love is better known through me. I believe this message not only prepared me to lose my job, but also is preparing me for whatever comes next vocationally.

Refining is hard. But, indeed, it is good.

We all lose our way from time to time. Suffering in particular will cause us to lose our way, as we feel deep things like grief and fear that blind us during our journey. Whether it's though a book, an experience, or someone we know, God comes and speaks to us to let us know we've lost our way. God still sends messengers like Malachi—such as when my boss at Mercer put me in my place. I'm sure we can all think of people who spoke hard truths in our lives, Malachis for us. We need those messages; we need to get called back to basics and deeper into relationship with God.

Losing our way is part of the natural course of life. And it's why we need to consistently be engaged in the process of sanctification: spending time with God, opening our hearts by praying with emotional honesty, and being willing to hear the hard messages that will free us from what binds.

While suffering, if we should choose to focus on what lasts, as Thompson says, on what really matters in life, we will take advantage of the tremendous opportunity God gives us. Suffering brings refinement, if we accept it, if we invite the suffering to pull up a chair to the table of our hearts. The tremendous change wrought by suffering can cause such refinement if we will cede to it. In fact, suffering is a messenger, a Malachi, in and of itself, and if we will listen to it, suffering will, "help us unlock the best of ourselves that hides in places we can't otherwise find."[36]

Refining is hard, but it is good.

C. S. Lewis perhaps put it best. The times of refinement are hard, he notes; they can feel like times of trouble and anguish, and he wonders aloud why we would need, as Christians, to go through these things. Lewis certainly wondered aloud why we would suffer. But then, he answers his own question this way, "It seems to us all unnecessary: but that is because we have not yet had the slightest notion of the tremendous things God means to make of us."

The tremendous things God means to make of us. God makes something tremendous of us, if only we will submit to being refined.

Our lives are but vapor: here for a minute and then gone. In that infinitesimal span of time, God sends us messages: to Malachi, to the people of God, to you, to me. God sends messages that call on us to grow in faith, to grow in love, to be refined.

Suffering is hard, but it creates tremendous opportunity to focus on what truly matters in this life to become the tremendous thing God means to make.

Field Notes

In this time of suffering, or in a previous time of suffering, how have you experienced God refining you? How has suffering revealed what truly matters in your life?

Chapter 20

Raise Your Ebenezer

"The same night he got up and took his two wives, his two maids, and his eleven children and crossed the ford of the Jabbok. He took them and sent them across the stream, and likewise everything that he had. Jacob was left alone, and a man wrestled with him until daybreak. When the man saw that he did not prevail against Jacob, he struck him on the hip socket, and Jacob's hip was put out of joint as he wrestled with him. Then he said, 'Let me go, for the day is breaking.' But Jacob said, 'I will not let you go, unless you bless me.' So he said to him, 'What is your name?' And he said, 'Jacob.' Then the man said, 'You shall no longer be called Jacob, but Israel, for you have striven with God and with humans and have prevailed.' Then Jacob asked him, 'Please tell me your name.' But he said, 'Why is it that you ask my name?' And there he blessed him. So Jacob called the place Peniel, saying, 'For I have seen God face to face, yet my life is preserved.' The sun rose upon him as he passed Penuel, limping because of his hip. Therefore to this day the Israelites do not eat the thigh muscle that is on the hip socket, because he struck Jacob on the hip socket at the thigh muscle."—Genesis 32:22-32

JUST A FEW WEEKS AGO, Carter and I drove around the Tuckasegee River looking for rocks. In particular, we wanted rocks of various sizes that could be glued together. At the time, it was just the two of us at the cabin, but we knew Jackson and Dana would arrive the next day. As we drove, we happened upon a spot where Carter eyed some rocks. Together, we loaded twelve into the bed of my truck.

The next day, we showed our haul to Jackson and Dana. Carter proudly displayed the epoxy glue we'd purchased, knowing it was his job to glue the rocks together. We declared to Jackson and Dana that we intended to build an Ebenezer, a word you may recall from the introduction that means "stone of help." In Jackson's continued illness, in the ways Carter has experienced the sorrow and worry that often envelop our house, in Dana's long-suffering care for us, and in my ongoing battles with primary immunodeficiency, we felt that we needed to raise an Ebenezer—a tangible sign of God's faithfulness to us.

We chose a spot near two other significant markers. On the left of the Ebenezer, just down a hillside, is a magnolia tree. Our dear friends we bonded with in Virginia gave us that tree when we lost a baby to miscarriage. Then, at the bottom of the hillside off to the right of the Ebenezer lies the spot where we spread the ashes of our first family dog, Lily. In our grief in those moments, we experienced God's presence, inspiring our hope. So just as discussed in Chapter 15, we looked to the past to find hope for the future, confident that in erecting this Ebenezer, we would look back on it at future moments, reminded of how God brought us through this challenging season of suffering.

In the classic hymn, "Come, Thou Fount of Every Blessing," we hear this line: "Here I raise mine Ebenezer; hither by thy help I'm come."[37] To raise an Ebenezer is to mark a moment where hope has triumphed over despair, where God has come through after a period of wrestling.

And while the word Ebenezer doesn't appear in the scripture of Jacob wrestling, I couldn't help but think of erecting stones of help as I revisited this famous scene from scripture.

Jacob has been striving, wrestling with life, for a while. He got jealous of his older brother Esau and tricked his father, Isaac, into giving him the birthright, rather than Esau who was supposed to receive it as the oldest child. He then gets tricked himself by Laban, the father of the woman whom he wants to marry, Rachel. Instead, he ends up marrying both sisters, having to work a total of fourteen years for Laban before finally getting the woman of his dreams in marriage.

Having so married, he sets off to build a life with his wives and the wealth gained from their dowries. But he finds out that Esau is looking for him. He thinks Esau is very angry and looking to destroy his brother and take back the birthright that was rightfully his. Jacob eventually turns to face Esau, choosing to meet him, and it's on the way to meet Esau that we find Jacob, alone, with his family and household on the other side of a river from him.

Jacob, we don't know why, has decided to stay on this side of the river by himself. Maybe he needed some introvert space to think through things. That's what I would need, considering all the striving and wrestling he's had going on in his life.

He's been through a series of hardships, some brought on by his own bad actions. If not for stealing the birthright, his brother wouldn't be angry and looking for him. Then, there are other hardships brought on by the bad actions of others: Laban tricking him into marrying Leah before Rachel. And undoubtedly, he had some wounds of his own, what the Enneagram refers to as the shadow side: the ways scars of old or unresolved issues can drive us and cause us to act in poor ways as we struggle within ourselves.

We can certainly relate to that kind of life. We recall times where we have struggled with hardships we brought upon ourselves. Perhaps we said something to someone we later regretted. Perhaps we did something to someone we later regretted. Perhaps we did something that caused harm to others. Perhaps it was something else.

Then consider times where something has happened in life that caused you to struggle. Perhaps it's being tricked by someone, like Jacob by Laban. Perhaps it's just because of something that happened in life: a health scare or hard diagnosis, a financial threat, a tragedy. These we can broadly characterize as suffering.

In both cases, we can find ourselves wrestling internally, struggling to understand what's going on, why it happened, and how we're supposed to respond. Then, it can go deeper. Prior to this moment in scripture, Jacob is talking to God, hoping God will provide but clearly wrestling in his relationship with God. He's deeply concerned about his very angry brother approaching him, thinking that will mean his destruction. Why would God allow this to happen? Hadn't he been faithful since his dastardly act of stealing the birthright? Crises in life—whether we bring them upon ourselves, they're caused by someone else, or they just happen—can lead to crises of faith. Why would a good God allow this bad thing to happen to a faithful person? Why is there still evil in the world if Jesus Christ came and, as said in communion liturgies, "Defeated sin and death, destroying their power forever"?

These are natural questions, things we ask ourselves, a wrestling we do when bad things happen. Jacob's there in his soul. And maybe that's why he stays alone, not crossing the river. Maybe he needs to think and sort things out.

The hymn, "Come, Thou Fount of Every Blessing," speaks to the wrestling that comes with the life of faith. "Prone to wander, Lord, I feel it, prone to leave the God I love,"[38] the author Robert Robinson writes. Indeed, when he speaks to the Ebenezer he raises, it's because "hither by [God's] help I come." He recognizes that it's through God's help he's come through the difficult circumstances, the struggles and challenges, the wrestling. And he both praises God for that deliverance and asks that he not wander again, not need to wrestle again.

We can relate. The life of faith is sometimes a life of wrestling: wrestling with the consequences of things we've done, wrestling with the consequences of the things others have done, wrestling with the bad things that happen in life, wrestling with our wounds and shadow side, and above all wrestling with the tough questions of faith. Why God, why?

I can hear Jacob asking that question as he remains alone on the bank of the river. In my mind's eye, I see him settling in to sleep when this man comes to wrestle with him until daybreak. He wrestles and wrestles and seems to have the upper hand until the man strikes his hip and puts it out of socket. This man clearly is no ordinary man, a man the scripture gradually reveals as God himself. Then God seems to have the upper hand in the wrestling but it's not over yet. God asks to be let go. But rather than give in, Jacob does this incredible thing. He says, "I will not let you go unless you bless me."

I will not let you go unless you bless me.

How often is it the case that when we have wrestlings in our souls, we are tempted to give in? Tempted to walk away? Decide that faith isn't worth it, that God isn't good, that a good God would not have allowed this thing to happen to me? Perhaps we have given in, deciding that a good God would not allow these things to happen and so maybe God doesn't exist or maybe God isn't for us but against us, or maybe God just doesn't care.

I've been there. Part of why I left faith in my mid-twenties was the thought that, if God was so good, there wouldn't be the suffering I knew, both internally and in the lives of those around me. If God really provided, I thought, there wouldn't be these hardships. I could never convince myself that God didn't exist, so I adopted a posture that said it didn't matter if God existed or not. God wasn't good, and so a life of faith was pretty well pointless.

In the internal wrestling I was doing, I had given in.

Maybe you can relate. Maybe you have friends or family members who are there. Perhaps they've had bad experiences with people of faith, or perhaps they were hurt by an experience at a church, or maybe they just have had some tough things happen in life and they've given in to the wrestling. Maybe that's been true for you. When facing this kind of internal wrestling, this suffering, it's tempting and even easy to give in.

But not Jacob. He's facing that kind of internal wrestling. He's wrestling with his faith, with God, but he won't give in. I will not let you go unless you bless me.

Robert Robinson wrestled for twenty-seven years. He was apprenticed to a hairdresser but didn't want that to be his career. He wrestled with that. He tried to understand the divine, feeling a sense of longing for faith, and tried various things, including seeing a fortune teller. He wrestled with God, too. One day, he heard George Whitefield preach. This was the same Whitefield who was a contemporary of John Wesley and helped found the Methodist movement. It was in hearing Whitefield's preaching that Robinson felt his twenty-seven years of wrestling come to an end. He felt blessed by what he heard, and he felt a resolution to his wrestling. And he then went and became a minister, serving several parishes and writing hymns. Robinson didn't give in. For twenty-seven years he kept wrestling. And God blessed him.

Jacob didn't give in. For many years, he kept wrestling. And God blessed him.

In the midst of my own wrestling, I have often spoken to God similarly to Jacob: I won't stop wrestling until you've completed your work. I will not let you go unless you bless me. I demand that God bring to completion what God had begun in my internal wrestling, in this season of suffering. I am doing what Jacob does here in the scripture.

And that makes all the difference.

Wrestling comes with the life of faith, just as we've noted that suffering comes with the life of faith. Deep, hard, internal struggles are a part of living the life of faith as we grow in our relationship with God. And when we encounter such wrestling, we should be bold like Jacob, saying to God that we will not give in, we will not let go, we will continue to wrestle, until God has blessed us.

Think back in your life to wrestlings that are now done. We all have those: Times when we can see how God blessed us because of the wrestling. Times when we can see how God came through and how we're now better and able to bless others because of the wrestling we did. I have heard powerful testimony from cancer survivors who, feeling blessed by their survival, are the greatest blessing to those who have recently received cancer diagnoses as they walk that journey together. The power of twelve-step programs comes through in sponsors. Those who have wrestled with their addictions choose to walk the path with those who are just starting the journey of addiction, bringing the blessing of their recovery to someone just beginning.

Jacob was blessed through his wrestling. Through him, the nation of Israel was born. Through him, God continued fulfillment of God's promise to his grandfather, Abraham. Through Jacob, now renamed Israel, the people of God were blessed.

We are blessed to be a blessing. And blessing is what can come through from a period of wrestling, from a hardship that has caused us to question our faith and question God's character. It's tempting to give in during those times of wrestling, times of suffering. Those are very difficult times indeed.

Jacob shows us that when wrestling deeply, internally, when struggling with God, don't give in until God has blessed you. Be bold like Jacob and demand a blessing.

For a blessing will come. A special imparting of God's grace will come as a result of our wrestling. As Paul says in Philippians, "I am confident of this, that the one who began a good work in you will continue to complete it until the day of Jesus Christ" (Philippians 1:6). At the end, we will know God better and we will be more effective witnesses for the gospel of Jesus Christ. At the end of our wrestling, we will be able to help others who are beginning the same journey through hardship. At the end, God will be able to do more through us. The wrestling will come to a completion. A blessing will come. And God will use that blessing to bless others.

The task for us, in the midst of wrestling, is to be bold like Jacob, to demand a blessing and don't stop wrestling until it comes.

That's hard, though. It's really hard. How do we find encouragement in the midst of wrestling?

At home, a glass ball the size of a cantaloupe sits on top of the piano. Every January and February, Jekyll Island hides plastic balls around the island and invites the public to come on a scavenger hunt for them. Many years now, we have gone down and done the scavenger hunt but never found one. Several years ago, we went to do the scavenger hunt as a way to get away after I had finished a particular period of wrestling. It was great to get out of town and get some good time in with family, marking the end of that wrestling and noting the ways I felt God had blessed me as a result of the suffering.

On the way off the island, we stopped at the visitor's center by the toll booths. If you find one of the plastic balls, they give you one of these glass balls for free. But, of course, they sell them, too. I'd always admired them. Dana went in and told me to pick one out. She wanted to get one to mark this moment of blessing, this end to my wrestling, this big moment in my personal development.

So I picked one out. It's not made of stone but it's still an ebenezer for me: a symbol of hope. When I have wrestled in the years since, just like this latest time these last few weeks, it has reminded me that God is good to complete the work God started: that a blessing will come from my wrestling. It's encouragement to not give in.

Now, the actual stone Ebenezer at our cabin will function in the same way. And, of particular importance, raising an Ebenezer while suffering is an act of defiance and hope—defiance in the face of the despair and fear that cling too closely, hope that our current circumstances and all the emotional and spiritual upheaval will not have the final word. God gets to have that.

To raise an Ebenezer is to issue a declaration: This suffering will not have the final word.

This is why Ebenezers are important. They remind us of when God has been faithful through our wrestling in the past. They serve as markers in our lives. They are acts of defiance. When Jacob names the spot of his wrestling Peniel, he's marking that space as a symbol of hope—an Ebenezer.

God is faithful. The good work being done in you through the wrestling will come to completion. You will be blessed. Just don't let go! Keep wrestling, keep walking through the land of suffering. Build or find an Ebenezer, something you can look to as a symbol in your current bout of suffering.

Let us raise our Ebenezers, for there is hope no matter our wrestling.

Field Notes

What item(s) are Ebenezers in your life? How might you raise an Ebenezer during this time of suffering?

PART 3

Discovering Hope

*This is a day of new beginnings, time to remember and move on,
time to believe what love is bringing, laying to rest the pain that's gone.*

*For by the life and death of Jesus, God's mighty Spirit, now as then,
can make for us a world of difference, as faith and hope are born again.*

*Then let us, with the Spirit's daring, step from the past and leave behind
our disappointment, guilt, and grieving, seeking new paths, and sure to find.*

*Christ is alive, and goes before us to show and share what love can do.
This is a day of new beginnings; our God is making all things new.*

—Brian Wren, 1978

Chapter 21

Find the Light

"In the beginning was the Word, and the Word was with God, and the Word was God. He was in the beginning with God. All things came into being through him, and without him not one thing came into being. What has come into being in him was life, and the life was the light of all people. The light shines in the darkness, and the darkness did not overtake it."—John 1:1-5

"Yet, in thy dark streets shineth the everlasting light."[39]

Phillips Brooks sat on horseback atop a hillside. This episcopal priest from New England had come to visit the Holy Land. As Christmas Eve approached, he journeyed out of Jerusalem toward Bethlehem, asking along the way where shepherds were keeping their flock by night. Locals pointed him toward a hilltop.

So it was that on Christmas Eve 1868, Brooks climbed the hill at night, looking at a brightly lit night sky. There were stars all around. And just off in the distance, the city of Bethlehem sat still, quiet, and dark.

This was long before electric lights illuminated homes and city streets in Bethlehem. The moment captured Brooks's imagination. He felt overcome by that rush of feeling we often attribute to the Holy Spirit. Brooks felt as though he was looking back in time, seeing things as they might have been for the shepherds.

When he got home to Boston, wanting to record his feelings, Brooks wrote a poem. He began, "O little town of Bethlehem, how still we see thee lie; above thy deep and dreamless sleep the silent stars go by."[40]

Brooks had experienced profound peace, profound silence, and the brilliance of a night sky unencumbered by artificial light. And so his poem continues: "Yet in thy dark streets shineth the everlasting light; the hopes and fears of all the years are met in thee tonight."[41]

In his powerful spiritual moment on that hillside looking at Bethlehem, Phillips Brooks knew this fundamental truth of our faith: No matter the darkness, the light shines.

Winston Churchill faced his own dark reality. The Nazis relentlessly bombed the cities of England. He and his companions were forced to take shelter multiple times just like so many of his fellow citizens. There was constant concern, especially for the prime minister's safety. It was with dismay and fear that, one day, an astute guard at the prime minister's weekend retreat noticed the roads around the retreat formed an unintentional bullseye when viewed from overhead, as if to lead German bombers directly to where Winston Churchill resided.

It was a dark hour in England's history; Churchill made no bones about that. His laments came forth in public speeches, helping the people to lament as well. He told them his longings, for peace and for an end to the war, not to pity himself nor the people but to encourage, to say that he longed, too, and that if they would embrace each other in their longings for peace, their longings for the light, they would make it through to the end.

One such speech came on Christmas Eve at the White House. Standing with President Franklin Roosevelt at the annual Christmas tree lighting ceremony, Churchill addressed the nation and the world. He gave a short speech, remarking via radio and to onlookers on the White House lawn, "Therefore, we may cast aside for this night at least the cares and dangers which beset us, and make for the children an evening of happiness in a world of storm. Here, then, for one night only, each home throughout the English-speaking world should be a brightly lighted island of happiness and peace."[42] It's easy to imagine that the lights of Washington, DC, and the Christmas tree moved Churchill as he saw the way the light shone in the darkness. Until his visit to DC, he had known only the darkness of night because of to the blackouts around his country.

The next morning, Churchill attended church with Roosevelt. There, they sang, "O Little Town of Bethlehem." As he sang, Churchill teared up as he heard these words from that carol, words that conveyed a meaning like his speech the night before: "Yet in thy dark streets shineth the everlasting light." No matter the darkness, the light shines.

The time of the writing of the Gospel of John was also a dark time. This is the newest of the gospels, written last, and written at least fifty years after Matthew, Mark, and Luke. By then, Christian persecution had picked up tremendously. Instead of persecution being regional, based on the sympathies of the governor of the region, the emperors themselves had taken up the cause of Christian persecution. As the faith spread like wildfire, the killings for entertainment, the imprisonments, and the executions picked up.

Christians longed for release from that persecution. They all knew someone who'd been jailed or executed or killed for sport in a stadium somewhere. They all had that personal, firsthand knowledge of death. And they longed to be released from it. Longing characterized the Christian people at this moment in history.

To write and disseminate a gospel at that time, then, was high treason—an act worthy of the worst persecution the Roman government could muster. It was at great personal risk that this gospel was not only written but passed around. It speaks of Jesus in a different way, captured here at the very beginning of creation. While Matthew, Mark, and Luke begin with Jesus's humanity, John begins with Jesus's divinity. He takes his cues from Genesis, noting that through Jesus, the divine Word as John calls him, all things were created and came into being.

For John's gospel, all life owes itself to Jesus. And that life Jesus brings is the light of the world: a light that the darkness did not and cannot overcome. That is John's central message. The darkness is all around these early Christians through persecution. And yet, they hear John say that the darkness did not overcome the light. His gospel is a word of encouragement to these persecuted Christians: No matter the darkness you know, no matter how much evil might seem to be winning, the light still shines. Jesus will not be defeated.

For John knew what Phillips Brooks and Winston Churchill discovered: "Yet in thy dark streets shineth the everlasting light." No matter the darkness, the light shines.

Standing in church during a dark Christmas season in my life, I heard that new Christmas carol I mentioned in Chapter 17, "I Want to Walk as a Child of the Light." As I heard those words, I couldn't help myself. Like Churchill hearing "O Little Town," I teared up. The chorus says, "In him there is no darkness at all. The night and the day are both alike. The Lamb is the light of the city of God. Shine in my heart, Lord Jesus."[43]

I needed the light so much that season. The darkness was all around me. Before that church service, I heard "the Christmas angels, their great glad tidings tell," as Phillips Brooks so poignantly wrote in "O Little Town," but their carols failed to resonate within me. The darkness was too great.

Perhaps you can relate. Darkness is often a metaphor for suffering. The journey through suffering, as we have seen, can often appear dark. Perhaps there's darkness from personal struggles, health issues, family drama, or friendship strife. Maybe there's darkness from impending threats to businesses or finances. Perhaps there is darkness from other places in our lives, but whatever the reason, perhaps you know darkness more than light this season. Perhaps you find yourself in a dark place.

A season of darkness was the kind of season I was having that particular year. I brought with me to church longings for peace, for release, for salvation from the workplace drama that engulfed me, and most of all, for a longing to come out of the fog of darkness and back into the light.

And then, this carol about light cut through the darkness and opened up my soul to see the light—to know that the light of Christ was still around me, still within me. I needed to know, again in my heart, that the light shines in the darkness and the darkness did not overcome it. In that hymn, I heard the assurance I needed.

Later that season, I heard "O Little Town" again but picked up on that line as never before: "Yet in thy dark streets shineth the everlasting light." And I knew, I just knew, that in my dark streets, the everlasting light was shining.

I knew it because I had given voice to my longings. And then, I found the light. Churchill gave voice to his longings, and then he found the light. The Apostle John gave voice to his longings and the longings of the early Christians, and then they, together, found the light. When we give voice to our longings, we find the light, for no matter the darkness, the light shines.

On a hillside similar to where Phillips Brooks sat that night in 1868, angels years before gave voice to the longings of the people of God as they told their great glad tidings to the shepherds keeping watch over their flock by night. And their tidings, their voice, showed the way to the light, for the shepherds and for the people of God forevermore.

That is the lesson for us as we move toward the close of this book. In all our stories and in the lyrics of these carols, we see this truth: Giving voice to our longings leads us to the light. For no matter the darkness, the light shines.

As you journey through the land of suffering, let yourself long for the light. Give voice to your longings: longings for peace in family drama or release from suffering, healing from a bad health diagnosis, recovery from a financial turnaround, release from the harmful actions of others or any number of ways we experience the darkness. Whether you know a little bit of darkness or the darkness seems overwhelming or somewhere in between, give voice to your longings.

Don't tune out the angels with their great glad tidings. Don't shut yourself off from others.

Instead, embrace your longings. For when we do, we open our souls up to receive the light of Christ. When we embrace our longings, when we learn to long for the light, we give God space to shine in our hearts, showing us that in Christ "there is no darkness at all. The night and the day are both alike." That no matter the darkness, the light shines.

This, then, is how we find hope while we walk through the land of suffering. We give voice to our longings. We tell God exactly what we want, what we need. As I journey myself, I do this frequently, sharing longings for restoration of my health and Jackson's, longings for lab results to return, longings to begin treatment, longings for a new job, longings to forgive those who harmed me and my family, longings for release from the anxiety and fear, all sorts of longings.

In sharing these longings with God, I give those longings to the one person who has the power to change things: God himself. There's power and release there, for in giving voice to our longings, we free ourselves from the pressure to have to solve our own problems. There, we find the hope we seek.

How do we give voice to our longings?

First, talk about them with friends and family. Don't keep them inside. That's the power of friendship. When we come to our friends and family with our longings, people we trust who will walk the journey of life with us, we meet Christ there in that relationship. Where two or three are gathered in Christ's name, Christ is there. And when we choose to be vulnerable and open about our longings with friends and family we trust, we find the light.

Second, talk with God about those longings. Pray with authentic longing. Just tell God what you're longing for. So often, we go in prayer to God and say to God what we think God wants to hear or what we think we're supposed to say. Just speak to God as you feel. If you have trouble finding the words, pray with scripture. You might also talk with your pastor or other spiritual advisor.

This, indeed, is what I am doing. In fact, at one of the last worship services I led, we sang this hymn, and with my voice cracking, I sang, "In him there is no darkness at all. The night and the day are both alike. The lamb is the light of the city of God. Shine in my heart, Lord Jesus." I felt the power, not only of the meaning of those words, but of reminding me how God had come through for me before. I found my hope renewed as I poured my longings into the singing of this hymn. When we pray with authentic longing, we can sing, "In him there is no darkness at all. The night and the day are both alike," and know, just know, that the light does indeed shine.

What are you longing for? Where do you know darkness? Give voice to those longings and you will find the light. "Yet in thy dark streets shineth the everlasting light. The hopes and fears of all the years are met in thee tonight."

No matter the darkness, the light shines.

Field Notes

What are you longing for? Today, through an act of prayer, give God those longings. This might look like taking a walk, prayer journaling, or singing a favorite hymn.

Chapter 22

Conclusion: God Empowers Us

"I greatly rejoice in the Lord, because you have finally renewed your interest in me. In fact, you were already interested, but you didn't have the opportunity to show it. I'm not saying this because I'm in need, because I've learned to adapt to any and all circumstances. I know what it is to be in need, and I know what it is to have plenty. I learned the secret of living contentedly in any and every situation, whether well fed, hungry, having a lot, or in need. I can do all things through Christ who strengthens me."
—Philippians 4:10-13, NVI-PT, translated from Portuguese

ONE NIGHT, several weeks ago, I learned a dear former professor of mine passed away unexpectedly. I had just wrapped up a time of prayer that evening, pouring out my longings for restoration and healing just as the previous chapter describes, leaving me feeling empty but more at peace. To help transition toward bed, I opened my phone and scrolled through Facebook, quickly learning this news.

This particular professor shaped my understanding of mission and evangelism. I went with him and several classmates to Venezuela for a missions course, learning about and supporting the work of a Methodist seminary there. Through these experiences, I became acquainted with both his scholarship and his heart. In his lived example, I saw not only a model for mission and evangelism, but I also saw a model for living life as a pastor and Christian.

As I scrolled through the comments, I saw where another professor had reposted a Facebook post from that same former professor. About a month earlier, as he lay in intensive care, he had posted a quote from Philippians 4, an English translation of his native Portuguese language. He shared that, despite his dire circumstances, he was finding peace and joy in the love of family and God. Then, he quoted a famous verse this way: "I have learned to adapt to all situations in life.' All my life, I have heard that verse as, "I have learned to be content with whatever I have." It turns out my former professor had one last witness for me.

In that witness, I have found much hope. As I have studied this passage from Philippians, I have clung ever more closely to it. There's tremendous hope here. As you read and conclude this book, I pray it will inspire hope for you no matter what the journey through the land of suffering holds.

Paul, as you may recall, is in prison. The church in Philippi has written to him to inquire as to how he's doing. This is one of the tricky things about interpreting Paul's letters. His letters are typically replies to letters he received—letters we do not have. But we can infer that the church in Philippi is very concerned about his condition and treatment in the prison.

They are concerned with good reason. Romans valued order very highly, so those considered to be disrupting the order of the empire were treated particularly poorly in prisons already considered to be poor. Paul has suffered greatly since his conversion on that Damascus Road, and now he suffers as he languishes in poor prison conditions. The church in Philippi is rightly concerned!

Yet Paul writes that he's learned, in the words of most English translations, to be content, whatever his circumstances. As I grew up, I heard this verse often quoted when I wanted something I could not have: a new toy, a video game, a car, any kind of material item. So until reading my professor's English translation of his Portuguese Bible, I had always considered this to be about finding contentment with current material possessions.

That, however, could not be further from the truth. Paul lived an itinerant lifestyle, staying with friends or hosted by churches he visited. With all his traveling, whether by foot on Roman roads or in ships, he would have packed light, having few materialistic possessions. Paul, at the time he wrote this, would not have referred to contentment with his materialistic possessions, as he lived a non-materialistic lifestyle!

He then further explains what he means by "content" in verse 12: "I I know what it is to be in need, and I know what it is to have plenty. I learned the secret of living contentedly in any and every situation, whether well fed, hungry, having a lot, or in need." Such writing refers not to material items but to the basics of life. Here he is in prison, probably poorly and perhaps not adequately clothed, shivering or sweltering with the weather, surviving off meager rations, perhaps suffering with disease or other maladies. Under such conditions, he has learned "the secret" of how to be "content."

Based on this, I think the Portuguese translation is better: Paul has learned to adapt to his ever-changing circumstances. Whether he's well-fed or not, whether he's shivering and sweltering or comfortable, whether he's healthy or racked by disease, he's learned to adapt such that he can say he is OK. Throughout this letter, which is indicative of all his letters, he shows much more concern for the people to whom he writes, like this church in Philippi, than he does for himself. While sitting in prison, almost certainly suffering, he says, "I want you to know, beloved, that what has happened to me has actually resulted in the progress of the gospel" (1:12). His primary concern remains the mission and supporting the churches who look to him for guidance.

So he has learned to adapt not simply to find peace and contentment but to continue the work to which God has called and equipped him. What an inspiring example of faith! In that example, I felt called, and inspired, to figure out how to adapt to my current circumstances. I wondered to myself how I could experience the peace, the contentment, the adaptation, that Paul describes here.

Because, as we've discussed at length in this book, journeying through the land of suffering brings discord, discontentment, and maladaptation. We find ourselves struggling mightily because of all the hardship, change, instability, and fear wrought by this journey. For me, understanding that Paul had learned to adapt, to cope, no matter his circumstances, gave me hope that I, too, could discover this "secret" that has given him peace and contentment, no matter what dire circumstances he knows.

In fact, such was part of what led to the writing of this book. A friend from Eastman, who heard many of my sermons, suggested I look back at all the ways I had taught her, and the congregation, to cope, or adapt, to times of suffering. As I looked back through sermons, I felt even more inspired to write this book. Many of those same sermons, now edited, comprise the chapters in Part 2. These are helpful to me, and I certainly hope you have found helpful practices to employ as you continue walking the journey of your own suffering. But as helpful as these practical tips for walking through the land of suffering may be, in studying Philippians I came to realize that Paul had found something deeper, something else I had not yet realized.

I wanted that deeper thing because, too often these last several months, I find myself feeling ushered into increasing darkness. I would employ many of these practices I have recommended to you yet felt my suffering growing. Losing my position at the church emphasized this reality. Whatever Paul had discovered, I needed it.

The very next verse, after he had expressed having found a secret, tells of that secret: "I can do all things through [Christ] who strengthens me" (Philippians 4:13). This very famous verse was so familiar to me that I had not paused to consider it in context: that this is the secret to which Paul refers, that Christ strengthens him to endure whatever life brings, whether for good or ill. That while we might quote it to ourselves or to a friend before a challenge, Paul means something deeper still: that we can adapt and find peace, regardless of our circumstances, because Christ strengthens us to do so.

This led me to wonder about that word "strengthen." It turns out it can also be translated as "empower," such that the verse would read (as some translations do), "I can do all things through Christ who empowers me." It might feel like semantics, but that word "empower" has a different connotation. Strengthening connotes the ability to stand up under a weight, holding things steady. Empowerment connotes the ability to do something about that weight, to respond to its proximate cause.

Empowerment spoke to my current circumstances. As I felt ushered into an increasing darkness, I felt increasingly powerless. It seemed I was a victim of my circumstances. As much as I tried, as much as I engaged the very practices I recommend to you, I felt more and more like a victim, unable to control anything at all, destined to suffer with no recourse.

Perhaps you can relate. It's easy while journeying through the land of suffering to feel victimized. In fact, we have learned together about the need to accept our circumstances and admit our powerlessness to get ourselves out of the land of suffering. Part of learning to cope, to adapt, involves accepting where we have power and where we do not. Only God can fully rectify the circumstances that led to our suffering. Restoration is in God's hands.

Yet that does not mean we are powerless, nor that we are victims to our suffering. We always retain control over how we respond to our circumstances.

Therein lies the secret Paul found, and tremendous hope for all of us as we journey through the land of suffering. God empowers our response to suffering circumstances. By drawing closer in our faith through practices like those outlined in Part 2, we find empowerment to adapt and, in our adaptations, find peace and contentment, regardless of our circumstances.

As this reality settled in, I thought about how I have responded and how I could respond. As just one example, I walked more than 250 miles in the last five months, for walking has proven helpful. Even when I do not feel well, I still force myself to get out and walk, knowing that it is good for my soul as well as my body. At the time I read my former professor's post, I thought about giving up walking, or at least walking less, feeling increasingly despondent. This said to me to keep going, that God empowered me to walk. And, as I considered this, God reminded me that often I find peace and new insight through walking. God used walking as empowerment for the journey.

Then, and perhaps most powerfully of all the thoughts I had, I heard God say to me to find joy in the mission. God has called us all to be witnesses, just like my former professor was even as he lay dying. While I am suffering in body, I am not dying just yet, so surely I could also find ways to witness. And not just ways to witness—ways to experience joy through laboring on behalf of the gospel, like Paul notes in Philippians 1. I prayed and asked God to reveal those ways to me, and one of them is this very book. God was faithful to answer, because God is faithful to empower.

I also engage in things that bring me joy, draw closer to friends and family, and engage in other practices just as I recommend to you throughout Part 2. In writing the first part, and now in writing this, I faced many challenging emotions, many difficult and hard things, and been overwhelmed by it. Yet I also experienced release in having to face those emotions and challenges, finding healing and further empowerment to keep going.

I write, and conclude, this book as one who has not yet finished the journey. At one point, I wondered to myself if such was a case of the blind leading the blind. I do experience blindness at times still as I journey, including just yesterday, forcing me to take a pause from writing. Yet I find empowerment, and increasingly so. I pray that in bearing witness to this empowerment, in bearing witness to my current suffering and in exposing past times of suffering, you will find empowerment, too, practicing faith in a way that draws you closer to God while journeying through the land of suffering.

In *The United Methodist Hymnal*, we omit a verse of Robert Robinson's from "Come, Thou Fount of Every Blessing," from which I got the title for this book. After the second verse, and before what the hymnal lists as the third, Robinson writes:

> Oh, that day when freed from sinning
> I shall see Thy lovely face
> Clothed then in blood washed linen
> How I'll sing Thy sovereign grace.
>
> Come my Lord, no longer tarry
> Take my ransomed soul away
> Send Thine angels now to carry
> Me to realms of endless days.[44]

Robinson certainly speaks of the eternal life we will know after meeting with death. And yet, I cannot help but hear the hope I long for in those last four lines, wishing for God to come quickly and send me to renewed days where I no longer suffer, for in "endless days" I hear days where suffering is ended. As we have seen, we know that God will do just this; suffering will not last forever, and God will "no longer tarry" but will bring us to "realms of endless days."

But until then, I will raise my Ebenezer. I will raise an Ebenezer of writing, finding joy in the mission. I will raise an Ebenezer of friends, finding comfort in their love. I will raise an Ebenezer of honest prayer, an Ebenezer of caring for others, an Ebenezer of focusing on what truly matters. God empowers me to raise these Ebenezers. In our physical Ebenezer we built, as I noted in chapter 20, we see a reminder that not only will God provide in the future, ending our suffering, but that God empowers us now, giving us what we need not only to adapt and cope, but perhaps even, to thrive despite our suffering.

In the end, this journey through the land of suffering is also a journey of discovery. As I lean into these practices, I discover God's faithfulness afresh and anew. As I pray and ask God to show me how God empowers me to live into the mission, even in my current condition, I discover new joys and challenges in my vocation. Even while walking this journey through the land of suffering, there are yet joys to be discovered, new ways to experience the love of God.

So raise your Ebenezer. Whether a physical, metaphorical, or both, through the practices listed here, raise your Ebenezer. Declare defiantly that God isn't done with you yet, that the suffering does not get to have the final word. God will make something tremendous of you yet. Find yourself on a journey of discovery. God empowers you, too, not to resolve your own suffering, but to adapt, finding the peace that Paul knew even in prison. If Paul can find his way to knowing inner peace, no matter his circumstances, we can, too. For God empowers us still today, so raise your Ebenezer.

As we close this book, I offer a common benediction I give when leading worship as my prayer for you, wherever you are on your own journey through the land of suffering:

> Then let us, with the Spirit's daring, step from our past and leave behind
> our disappointment, guilt, and grieving, seeking new paths and sure to find
> Christ is alive and goes before us, to show and share what love can do.
> This is a day of new beginnings! Our God is making all things new.[45]

Amen.

Field Notes

How is God empowering you as you journey through the land of suffering? What are you discovering? And, having considered the whole book, how can you raise your Ebenezer?

Afterword

AFTER SUBMITTING THIS MANUSCRIPT, I found myself often thinking of the parable of the lost sheep. My head frequently goes to scripture, and much of the time, it goes to the Old Testament. Perhaps this book makes evident that the Old Testament is my favorite, especially the wisdom literature of the Psalms and Ecclesiastes. But, in the last several months, this lost sheep and her shepherd kept coming to mind.

I sent the manuscript off to my excellent editor and publisher, Jessica Brodie, back in early July. At the time, our family stood at the cusp of significant changes. Just a few days after I sent off the manuscript, we finalized our decision to relocate permanently to our cabin in the mountains of Western North Carolina. God had made clear that no opportunity remained for us in Macon and, after a season of losing health, jobs, and the heartache of the loss of relationships, church, and stability, we felt God nudging us to start afresh and anew here at our cabin, in the place that feels the most at home for us.

We spent the last few months moving—gradually at first, but then rapidly as our house in Macon finally sold in November. At the same time, the boys worked to get established in new schools, making new friends, learning new systems. Dana started teaching high school, a first for her, and worked to get settled into not only a new school and school system, but a new state with differing standards and expectations.

During that time of change, we continued to wander through the land of suffering. I thought often of the words I wrote here, and the spiritual practices I recommended. The boys suffered mightily, each in their own way. Dana and I found ourselves suffering both from processing all we had experienced, all the change, but also from experiences of betrayal and financial loss that cascaded as summer turned to fall. The loss of health, job, and stability proved costly in more ways than one. As a family, we sat at the dinner table, sometimes utilizing Examen, sometimes just talking through our feelings, our experiences, as we continued to journey through the land of suffering. Ultimately, we practiced vulnerability, modeling it for each other.

The sheep in the parable is highly vulnerable. She's lost, missing, frightened. When this parable first started to come to mind over the summer, I identified with the sheep. I often felt alone and frightened, wondering where the shepherd was. Such is the land of suffering. As we have seen, finding ourselves there blinds, disorients, and leaves us wondering where God, our divine shepherd, is.

As I watched my family continue to suffer and as I worked through my own struggles, I continued to wonder when God would pull us through, and I kept thinking about the sheep. I felt us wandering, suffering, disoriented. Most of the summer and into the fall, Dana and I would remind ourselves that all we could do was figure out the next step, the next faithful step, and take it.

As I applied for jobs, one particular opportunity stood out. The application process took five weeks, and at the end of it, I had a job offer. Several other positions, for which I was highly qualified, had not panned out, but this one had. The company was enthusiastic about me, and I felt God nudging me in that direction. In late September, I accepted a job as a financial advisor.

The next several weeks, the light grew. I started to see what appeared to be a path forward. We settled into our lives. I continued to think about the sheep. Then, sitting at a great local wine bar before Thanksgiving, Dana helped me see what God had been doing. Back in January, as you read in chapter 19, God gave me new insight—what I now understand as a renewed sense of calling. I knew in January that God had called me to labor alongside others to promote financial freedom. I thought, at the time, it was a call to focus on fixing the finances at the church I served, setting the church free to put its energies elsewhere. Now I can see God preparing me for this new role, to work with individuals and organizations to gain firm financial footing so they can live out their lives without the burdens of financial stress and with a deeper spirit of kingdom-building generosity.

Suddenly, it all lined up. I remembered the wise voice of a spiritual director who said, a week after Mulberry voted me out, that she thought God had delivered me, but it just "looked a little funny." I remembered a dean and friend at the Candler School of Theology remarking to me about how losing his job at one point in his career and having to start over was "the best thing that could have happened." I considered this renewed sense of calling, and how it jibes with so much of what God has done in my life, and suddenly, my experience in the land of suffering made sense.

I thought again of the sheep. God had found me, just like the shepherd finding his lost sheep. I was lost but now was found. And turns out, back in January, God started preparing me for just what was to come. And then God sent prophets, wise voices, into my life to provide clarity and hope. Then God provided a job that made the pieces fit, gave us hope, and delivered us out of the land of suffering. Today, all four of us feel settled, renewed, redeemed, delivered out of the land of suffering. As the author Philip Yancey remarked in his book, *Disappointment with God*, "Faith means believing in advance what will only make sense in reverse." It makes sense today, but the trick, as we have seen throughout this book, is to believe in advance while going through hardship.

God prepared me, God restored my health and Jackson's, God delivered me from a toxic and unhealthy situation, and God restored our family and brought us home. In being lost, and now found, we feel once again at home. To be sure, home now is in North Carolina, not Georgia. Leaving home now means to work for a corporation, not a church, in the financial services industry, not in the world of nonprofits. But home is more than a place; it's where our hearts and souls find their rest. When in the land of suffering, our hearts and souls struggle to find rest, but now, having been found by God, we are once again at home.

I received the fullness of this message at the start of Advent, on the first Sunday in fact, when much of the Christian world lights the hope candle. There is hope, for God always comes to find us. From time to time, we will get lost in the land of suffering. But, "It is not the will of [our] Father in heaven that one of these little ones should be lost" (Matthew 18:14).

We will be found. There is always hope.

Ted Goshorn
Tuckasegee, North Carolina
Advent 2024

APPENDIX I

From Chapter 12

For Ted Goshorn
Short of Breath from Life's Exhaustion

Words and Music: Terre Johnson

Appendix 2

Thanksgiving Worksheet

From Chapter 15

Use the template provided here to construct your own version of Psalm 136, filling in the blanks with elements of your family's history. Perhaps do it together as a family and pray this as a prayer together; maybe do it individually as an act of devotion. However you do it, let it create for you a spirit of thanksgiving and an awareness that, in your family and with your loved ones, you have indeed known that God's steadfast love endures forever.

> O give thanks to the Lord, for he is good,
> for his steadfast love endures forever.
> O give thanks to the God of gods,
> for his steadfast love endures forever.
> O give thanks to the Lord of lords,
> for his steadfast love endures forever;
> who alone does great wonders,
> for his steadfast love endures forever;
> who by understanding made the heavens
> for his steadfast love endures forever;
> who _____

for his steadfast love endures forever;

for his steadfast love endures forever;

for his steadfast love endures forever;

for his steadfast love endures forever;

for his steadfast love endures forever;

for his steadfast love endures forever;

for his steadfast love endures forever;

for his steadfast love endures forever;

for his steadfast love endures forever;

for his steadfast love endures forever;

for his steadfast love endures forever;

for his steadfast love endures forever;

_____

for his steadfast love endures forever;

_____

for his steadfast love endures forever;

_____

for his steadfast love endures forever;

_____

for his steadfast love endures forever;

_____

for his steadfast love endures forever.

It is he who remembered us in our low estate,
for his steadfast love endures forever;
and rescued us from our foes,
for his steadfast love endures forever;
who gives food to all flesh,
for his steadfast love endures forever.
O give thanks to the God of heaven,
for his steadfast love endures forever.
Amen

Notes

Chapter 2
1. Stephen M.R. Covey, *The Speed of Trust: The One Thing that Changes Everything* (Free Press, 2006).

Chapter 3
2. Christina G. Rossetti, "In the Bleak Midwinter," *The United Methodist Hymnal* (The United Methodist Publishing House, 1989), 221.

Chapter 5
3. Jason Brian Santos, *A Community Called Taizé: A Story of Prayer, Worship and Reconciliation* (IVP Books, 2008).

4. Philip Yancey, *Disappointment with God: Three Questions No One Asks Aloud* (Zondervan, 1988).

5. Phillips Brooks, "O Little Town of Bethlehem," *The United Methodist Hymnal* (The United Methodist Publishing House, 1989), 230.

Chapter 6
6. Brian Wren, "This is a Day of New Beginnings," *The United Methodist Hymnal* (The United Methodist Publishing House, 1989), 383.

Chapter 8
7. C.S. Lewis, *The Silver Chair* (HarperTrophy, 2000).

Chapter 9

8. Joseph Mohr, "Silent Night, Holy Night," *The United Methodist Hymnal* (The United Methodist Publishing House, 1989), 239.

9. Ibid.

10. Scott Soper, "Child of the Poor," in *Voices Together* (MennoMedia, 2020), 268.

11. William C. Dix, "What Child Is This?" *The United Methodist Hymnal* (The United Methodist Publishing House, 1989), 219.

12. Ibid.

13. Soper, "Child of the Poor."

14. Mohr, "Silent Night."

15. Adolphe-Charles Adam. John S. Dwight, translator, "O Holy Night," in *African Methodist Episcopal Church Hymnal* (The African Methodist Episcopal Church, 2000), 121.

Chapter 10

16. Alexis Coe, *You Never Forget Your First: A Biography of George Washington* (Viking, 2020)

17. Yancey, *Disappointment with God.*

Chapter 11

18. See Appendix 1.

Chapter 12

19. Rossetti, "In the Bleak Midwinter."

20. Charles Wesley, "Come, Thou Long-Expected Jesus," *The United Methodist Hymnal* (The United Methodist Publishing House, 1989), 196.

21. Ibid.

22. Dwight, "O Holy Night."

23. Edmund H. Sears, "It Came upon a Midnight Clear," *The United Methodist Hymnal* (The United Methodist Publishing House, 1989), 218.

24. Dwight, "O Holy Night."

25. Wesley, "Come, Thou Long-Expected Jesus."

Chapter 13
26. Dennis Linn, Shiela Fabricant Linn, Matthew Linn, *Sleeping with Bread: Holding What Gives You Life* (Paulist Press, 1995).

Chapter 15
27. National Archives, "Transcript for President Abraham Lincoln's Thanksgiving Proclamation from October 3, 1863," accessed November 14, 2022, https://obamawhitehouse.archives.gov/sites/default/files/docs/transcript_for_abraham_lincoln_thanksgiving_proclamation_1863.pdf.

28. Henry Wadsworth Longfellow, "Christmas Bells," National Park Service, accessed November 14, 2022, https://www.nps.gov/long/learn/historyculture/christmas-bells.htm.

29. Ibid.

30. Joachim Neander, "Praise to the Lord, the Almighty," *The United Methodist Hymnal* (The United Methodist Publishing House, 1989), 139.

31. Longfellow, "Christmas Bells."

Chapter 17
32. Kathleen Thomerson, "I Want to Walk as a Child of the Light," *The United Methodist Hymnal* (The United Methodist Publishing House, 1989), 206.

Chapter 18
33. St. Francis of Assisi, William H. Draper, translator, "All Creatures of Our God and King," *The United Methodist Hymnal* (The United Methodist Publishing House, 1989), 62.

Chapter 19
34. Wright Thompson, *Pappyland: A Story of Family, Fine Bourbon, and the Things that Last* (Penguin Press, 2020).

35. Thompson, *Pappyland*.

36. Thompson, *Pappyland*.

Chapter 20

37. Robinson, "Come, Thou Fount of Every Blessing," *The United Methodist Hymnal* (The United Methodist Publishing House, 1989), 400.

38. Robinson, "Come, Thou Fount of Every Blessing."

Chapter 21

39. Brooks, "O Little Town."

40. Ibid.

41. Ibid.

42. David McCullough, *In the Dark Streets Shineth: A 1941 Christmas Eve Story* (Shadow Mountain Publishing, 2010).

43. Thomerson, "I Want to Walk as a Child of the Light."

Chapter 22

44. C. Michael Hawn, "History of Hymns, 'Come, thou Fount of every blessing," Discipleship Ministries, accessed April 24, 2024 https://www.umcdiscipleship.org/resources/history-of-hymns-come-thou-fount-of-every-blessing.

45. Brian Wren, "This is a Day of New Beginnings," *The United Methodist Hymnal* (The United Methodist Publishing House, 1989), 383.

About the Author

Dr. Ted Goshorn

Ted Goshorn lives, moves, and has his being in the mountains of Western North Carolina. There, with his wife, Dana, his sons Jackson and Carter, and his dog, Quill, they have found a deep sense of home after wandering through the land of suffering. Ted will soon serve as a financial advisor, working with individuals and communities to faithfully steward the resources entrusted to them. Ordained in The United Methodist Church, Ted holds a Doctor of Ministry from the Candler School of Theology at Emory University, along with various other degrees from Emory, James Madison University, and Berry College. He has inspired collaborations across religious, nonprofit, and government agencies; led efforts to pay off more than $1 million in medical debt; and fostered children and youth support programs. For his effort with at-risk youth, the Emory University Alumni Association recognized Ted as one of its 40 Under Forty in 2021. Ted wrote this book while in the land of suffering and prays it gives you hope as you seek God on your journey.

www.ingramcontent.com/pod-product-compliance
Lightning Source LLC
Chambersburg PA
CBHW050858160426
43194CB00011B/2204